Fortuna Fortes Sequitur

Ex Libris Lt.Col. Robert L. Turkoly-Joczik

VIETNAM STUDIES

COMMAND AND CONTROL 1950-1969

by

Major General George S. Eckhardt

DEPARTMENT OF THE ARMY
WASHINGTON, D.C. 1974

Library of Congress Catalog Card Number: 72-600186

Reprinted 1974

For sale by the Superintendent of Documents, U.S. Government Printing Office
Washington, D.C. 20402 - Price $1.80

Stock Number 008–020–00500–2/Catalog No. D 101.74:C73/2/950–69

Foreword

The United States Army has met an unusually complex challenge in Southeast Asia. In conjunction with the other services, the Army has fought in support of a national policy of assisting an emerging nation to develop governmental processes of its own choosing, free of outside coercion. In addition to the usual problems of waging armed conflict, the assignment in Southeast Asia has required superimposing the immensely sophisticated tasks of a modern army upon an underdeveloped environment and adapting them to demands covering a wide spectrum. These involved helping to fulfill the basic needs of an agrarian population, dealing with the frustrations of antiguerrilla operations, and conducting conventional campaigns against well-trained and determined regular units.

It is as always necessary for the U.S. Army to continue to prepare for other challenges that may lie ahead. While cognizant that history never repeats itself exactly and that no army ever profited from trying to meet a new challenge in terms of the old one, the Army nevertheless stands to benefit immensely from a study of its experience, its shortcomings no less than its achievements.

Aware that some years must elapse before the official histories will provide a detailed and objective analysis of the experience in Southeast Asia, we have sought a forum whereby some of the more salient aspects of that experience can be made available now. At the request of the Chief of Staff, a representative group of senior officers who served in important posts in Vietnam and who still carry a heavy burden of day-to-day responsibilities has prepared a series of monographs. These studies should be of great value in helping the Army develop future operational concepts while at the same time contributing to the historical record and providing the American public with an interim report on the performance of men and officers who have responded, as others have through our history, to exacting and trying demands.

All monographs in the series are based primarily on official records, with additional material from published and unpublished secondary works, from debriefing reports and interviews with key participants, and from the personal experience of the author. To facilitate security clearance, annotation and detailed bibliography have been omitted from the published version; a fully documented account with bibliography is filed with the Office of the Chief of Military History.

The reader should be reminded that most of the writing was accomplished while the war in Vietnam was at its peak, and the monographs frequently refer to events of the past as if they were taking place in the present.

Major General George S. Eckhardt has exceptional personal knowledge of command and control arrangements in Vietnam. In December 1966 he commanded the 9th Infantry Division and deployed it to South Vietnam. He commanded the division in combat until June 1967 when he was assigned as Deputy Commanding General, II Field Force, Vietnam. In January 1968 he became the Commanding General of the Delta Military Assistance Command and Senior Advisor, IV Corps Tactical Zone, with headquarters in Can Tho, Republic of Vietnam, and remained in these positions until the summer of 1969. The author returned to Vietnam in April 1971 as Special Assistant to the Deputy Commander, MACV, for Civil Operations and Rural Development Support (CORDS).

Washington, D.C.
15 January 1973

VERNE L. BOWERS
Major General, USA
The Adjutant General

Preface

In combat situations prior to Vietnam, U.S. military forces had an existing command and control structure which could be tailored to accomplish the task at hand. In Europe during World War II General Dwight D. Eisenhower modified the command structures developed for the North African and Mediterranean operations to form Supreme Headquarters, Allied Expeditionary Force (SHAEF). After his departure from Bataan in 1942, General Douglas MacArthur had several months in which to design the command structure that ultimately contributed to the defeat of the Japanese. Finally, the U.S. Eighth Army, the dominant command structure controlling all UN forces in combat in Korea, and the General Headquarters, United Nations Command, in Japan, existed prior to the beginning of the Korean War. Such was not the case in Vietnam. There, the command and control arrangements, which ultimately directed a U.S. military force of over 500,000 men, evolved from a small military assistance mission established in 1950. The Military Assistance Advisory Group's philosophy of assistance rather than command significantly influenced the development of the organization.

This monograph describes the development of the U.S. military command and control structure in Vietnam. The focus of the study is primarily on the Military Assistance Command, Vietnam (MACV), and the U.S. Army in Vietnam (USARV). The relationships with the Joint Chiefs of Staff (JCS), Commander in Chief, Pacific (CINCPAC), U.S. Army, Pacific (USARPAC), and other outside agencies are discussed only as their decisions, policies, and directives affected MACV and operations within South Vietnam. The air war against North Vietnam and naval operations of the U.S. Seventh Fleet were CINCPAC's responsibilities and are only mentioned in regard to their impact on MACV and the forces under MACV.

This study is not a conventional military or diplomatic history of the war in Vietnam. Rather, it is an analytical appraisal of the command and control structure.

There is no single study of command and control in Vietnam in existence. Several primary sources cover particular time periods,

v

and special studies provide selective but restricted coverage. The command histories of MACV and CINCPAC are useful references. The end-of-tour reports of senior military officials who served in Vietnam, particularly the combined end-of-tour reports of Admiral U.S. Grant Sharp and General William C. Westmoreland, add further depth.

The histories of the United States Army, Pacific, and United States Army, Vietnam, provided additional information, as did the special reports of the 1st Logistical Command. Data furnished by the Armed Forces Staff College and the Command and General Staff College provided material for the section on current doctrine for unified commands. The official histories of World War II and Korea, prepared by the Office, Chief of Military History, offer useful comparisons with the history of earlier unified commands.

In researching and writing this monograph the author received assistance from many organizations and individuals.

The Deputy Commandant of the U.S. Army War College, Brigadier General Wallace C. Magathan, Jr., provided the author with much backup material and acted as an assistant from the inception of this monograph to its completion. Major General Charles J. Timmes (Retired) provided a valuable service in checking the monograph for accuracy concerning the period when he was the Chief, Military Assistance Advisory Group. The Office, Chief of Military History, provided advice and sources of information, made available unpublished documents and data relating to U.S. military activities in Vietnam, and assisted in preparing photographs, maps, and charts.

The cheerful and efficient documentary research assistance of Miss Carmen Clark of the U.S. Army War College Library relieved the staff of much tedious work. Also, the U.S. Army War College Library under the direction of Miss Ruth Longhenry provided an ideal atmosphere for the research and writing.

The Strategic Studies Institute of the U.S. Combat Developments Command at Carlisle Barracks gave its support, and the contributions of Colonel Ralph T. Tierno, Jr., of that organization were noteworthy.

Major Paul L. Miles, Jr., Office, Chief of Staff, U.S. Army, was most co-operative and helpful in making available much primary source material.

Thanks are due also to Colonel John P. Lucas, Jr., of the Staff and Faculty, Armed Forces Staff College, and to Lieutenant Colonel Lloyd R. Kelly, Staff and Faculty, Command and General Staff College, for their contribution of research material.

A particular debt of gratitude is owed the twenty-six senior military and civilian officials for taking time from their busy schedules to answer the questionnaire related to this study.

Another contributor to the successful completion of this monograph was Mrs. Donna L. Moyer, whose tasks were keeping records, assisting with the organization, preparing associated correspondence, and typing many of the various drafts. She was ably assisted by the members of the U.S. Army War College typing pool headed by Mrs. June L. Rhoads.

Finally, special debts of gratitude are owed to a member of the U.S. Army War College faculty, Colonel James M. McGarity, who acted as a team chief for the preparation of the monograph, and to five members of the Class of 1971 of that college who, as members of the team, devoted considerable time in helping him with the research and writing. They are Colonel Leslie D. Carter, Colonel Charles J. Bauer, Colonel Duane H. Smith, Lieutenant Colonel William C. Rousse, and Lieutenant Colonel William P. Snyder.

Saigon, Vietnam
1 December 1972

GEORGE S. ECKHARDT
Major General, U.S. Army

Contents

Charts

Map

Illustrations

Illustrations are from Department of Defense files except the pictures on pages 48, 65, and 69, which are from Department of State files.

COMMAND AND CONTROL
1950–1969

NORTH VIETNAM

DEMARCATION LINE

QUANG TRI
Quang Tri ⊛

HUE ⊛
THUA THIEN

MUI DA NANG
DA NANG

QUANG NAM   Hoi An ⊛
I CORPS

Tam Ky ⊛

QUANG TIN

Quang Ngai ⊛
QUANG NGAI

THAILAND

KONTUM

⊛ Kontum   BINH DINH

DINH

Pleiku ⊛
PLEIKU   ⊛ Qui Nhon

PHU BON
Hau ⊛ Bon   PHU YEN

C A M B O D I A   BON   Tuy Hoa ⊛

II CORPS

DARLAC

⊛ Ban Me Thuot   KHANH HOA

HOA   ⊛ Nha Trang

QUANG DUC   TUYEN DUC
Gia Nghia ⊛   DA LAT ⊙
NINH THUAN   CAM RANH
PHUOC
Phuoc ⊛ Binh
BINH   An ⊛   LONG   LAM DONG   Tong Nghia ⊛
TAY NINH   Bao Loc ⊛   Phan Rang ⊛
Tay Ninh ⊛   LONG
III CORPS   BINH THUAN

BINH   LONG   BINH
DUONG   KHANH   BINH THUAN
Phu   BIEN   TUY
Cuong   Bien ⊛
MAU   HOA   Xuan Loc ⊛
Khiem ⊛   Loc   Phan Thiet ⊛
NGHIA   SAIGON   ⊛ Ham Tan
KIEN   Moc   LONG AN   GIA   PHUOC
Chau   PHONG   Hoa   DINH   TUY
CHAU   Phu   Cao Lanh ⊛   DINH Tan   GO CONG
DOC   AN   SA   VINH   Truc Giang ⊛   VUNG TAU   CAPITAL
Long   DEC   Long ⊛   KIEN HOA   SPECIAL ZONE
Xuyen   GIANG   GO CONG
DAO   KIEN   Rach Gia ⊛   Phu Vinh ⊛
PHU QUOC   GIANG   PHONG   VINH
(Vietnam)   DINH   BINH
(KIEN GIANG)   Thanh   Phu Vinh
CHUONG   BA   VINH
HON   THIEN   XUYEN   BINH
PANJANG   Khanh   Hung ⊛
Quan   BAC   IV CORPS
Long ⊛   LIEU   Bac Lieu ⊛
AN
XUYEN

MUI BAI BUNG   CON SON
(Administered from Saigon)

SOUTH VIETNAM
ADMINISTRATIVE DIVISIONS
AND MILITARY REGIONS
JULY 1968

------- International boundary
——— Province boundary
≡≡≡≡≡ Military corps boundary
⊛ National capital
⊙ Province capital
DA LAT Autonomous municipality

0   25   50   75   100 Miles
0   25   50   75   100 Kilometers

BOUNDARY REPRESENTATION IS
NOT NECESSARILY AUTHORITATIVE

Source: 1969 Summary, USMACV, published by the Office of Information, USMACV. Saigon: 15 February 1970.

CHAPTER I

The Formative Years: 1950–1962

Introduction

In 1950 the United States began to grant military aid to the French forces in Indochina in an effort to avert a Communist take-over of Laos, Cambodia, and Vietnam. From that time U.S. military assistance, adapted to the increasing Communist threat, developed in three phases: military advice and assistance; operational support of the South Vietnamese armed forces; and, finally, the introduction of U.S. combat forces. The U.S. armed forces in each of these phases were fulfilling their mission under the U.S. policy of ensuring the freedom of Indochina and specifically the freedom of South Vietnam.

The direction, control, and administration of U.S. armed forces throughout this period of U.S. commitment initially was vested in a military assistance advisory group and, beginning in 1962, in the Military Assistance Command, Vietnam. Both headquarters had joint staffs with representatives from all the armed services. Since the U.S. Army had the largest share of the mission of advising, training, and supporting the South Vietnamese armed forces, U.S. Army representation on the joint staffs and in the field was proportionately greater than that of the other services. The U.S. Army also provided the commanders of the Military Assistance Advisory Group and the Military Assistance Command, Vietnam.

The U.S. Military Assistance Command, Vietnam, was a unified command, more specifically a subordinate unified command, under the Commander in Chief, Pacific. Precedents for such an arrangement are found in the command and control structures of World War II. Lessons from that experience played an important role in establishing the doctrine for unified commands that, with modifications, was applied to the Korean War and the Vietnam conflict.

Joint Doctrine for Unified Commands

A unified command is a joint force of two or more service components under a single commander, constituted and designated by the Joint Chiefs of Staff. Generally, a unified command will have a broad, continuing mission that requires execution by significant forces of two or more services under single strategic direction. This was the case in South Vietnam.

The current doctrine for unified commands is based on the National Security Act of 1947, which authorized the establishment of unified commands in the U.S. armed forces. In 1958 an amendment to the act authorized the President to establish unified commands to carry out broad and continuing operations. Developing doctrine concerning the organization and operations of U.S. unified commands is the responsibility of the Joint Chiefs of Staff. The "JCS Unified Command Plan" and *JCS Publication 2: United Action Armed Forces (UNAAF)* provide the guidelines governing the responsibilities of commanders in unified (multiservice) and specified (single service) forces. These publications include doctrine for unified operations and training.

The three military departments, under their respective service secretaries, organize, train, and equip forces for assignment to unified and specified commands. It is also the responsibility of the departments to give administrative and logistical support to the forces assigned to the unified commands. One of the primary functions of the Department of the Army, for example, is to organize, train, and equip Army forces for the conduct of prompt and sustained combat operations on land in order to defeat enemy land forces and to seize, occupy, and defend land areas.

Effective application of military power requires closely integrated efforts by the individual services. It is essential, therefore, that unity of effort is maintained throughout the organizational structures as well. This goal is achieved through two separate chains of command—operational and administrative. Operational control runs from the President to the Secretary of Defense to the Joint Chiefs of Staff to the unified commands. The administrative-logistical chain of command runs from the President to the Secretary of Defense to the secretaries of the military departments and then to the service components of the unified commands.

The Joint Chiefs of Staff have defined the duties of unified and specified commanders who use the forces provided by the military departments. The Joint Chiefs establish policy concerning the command, organization, operations, intelligence, logistics, and administration of service forces and their training for joint operations. These guidelines also apply to subunified commands.

Army doctrine for unified commands is set forth in *FM 100–15: Larger Units, Theater Army Corps* (December 1968). In this document, Army policy governing command in a theater of operations during wartime varies from that presented by the Joint Chiefs. According to the Joint Chiefs, the unified commander does not additionally serve as a commander of any service component or another subordinate command unless authorized by the establishing authority. Current Army doctrine states:

> During peacetime the theater *army* commander normally commands all Army troops, activities, and installations assigned to the theater. [However] . . . during wartime, the theater commander normally withdraws from the theater army commander operational control of army combat forces, theater army air defense forces, combat support forces, and other specified units required to accomplish the theater operational mission. The theater commander, therefore, normally exercises operational command of most tactical ground forces during wartime. . . . Exceptionally, during wartime the theater commander may direct the theater army commander to retain operational control of US ground force operations. In this instance, the theater army commander provides strategic and tactical direction to field armies and other tactical forces.

Both doctrines, however, agree that the commander of a subordinate unified command set up by a unified command with approval of the Secretary of Defense has responsibilities, authorities, and functions similar to those of the commander of a unified command, established by the President.

Component and subunified commands are subordinate to the unified command in operational matters. In other words, the unified commander has operational command of these elements. The term "operational command" applies to the authority exercised by the commanders of unified commands. It is also used in other command situations such as combined commands. No commander is given more authority than he needs to accomplish his mission. The unified commander's instructions may be quite specific; the component commander, however, is usually given sufficient latitude to decide how best to use his forces to carry out the missions and tasks assigned to him by the unified commander. The subunified commander has the same authority as a unified commander over the elements in his command. The structure and organization of a subunified command are determined by the missions and tasks assigned to the commander, the volume and scope of the operations, and the forces available. With these factors in mind, the organization of a subunified command should be designed on the principles of centralized direction, decentralized execution, and common doctrine. Thus the integrity of the individual services is preserved.

The Beginning of U.S. Support to Vietnam

The U.S. command and control organization for directing and administering American military assistance for Vietnam was influenced by World War II and Korean precedents. The origins of American military assistance policies developed after World War II are found in the aggressive expansionist policies of the USSR and the need to strengthen the free nations of the world, whose security was vital to the United States. Out of the U.S. resolve to assist the Free World grew the North Atlantic Treaty Organization (NATO) in 1949 and the Southeast Asia Treaty Organization (SEATO) in 1954, established after France had lost in Indochina. Since U.S. military assistance to Indochina in general and to Vietnam in particular was channeled through France during the first Indochina War (1946–1954), French influence was felt strongly in the early 1950s and also had its effect on the organization and operation of the U.S. Military Assistance Group in Indochina.

Military assistance after World War II was authorized on a regional, comprehensive scale by the Mutual Defense Assistance Act of 6 October 1949. Its chief objective was to strengthen the North Atlantic Treaty Organization, in which France was a key member. At the time, France was heavily engaged in the first Indochina War and U.S. military assistance to Southeast Asia began to increase steadily. To supplement military assistance with economic aid, the U.S. Congress a year later sanctioned technical aid to underdeveloped nations by passing the Act for International Development, popularly known as the Point Four Program. In 1951 the two acts, along with other similar measures, were consolidated in the Mutual Security Act, which was revised again in 1953 and 1954 to meet the needs of the expanding Mutual Security program. An essential condition to be met before U.S. assistance could be given under this legislation was the conclusion of bilateral agreements between the United States and the recipient nation, which included the assurances that assistance would be reciprocal, that any equipment and information furnished would be secured, and especially that equipment would not be retransferred without U.S. consent.

Since it was the policy of the United States to support the peaceful and democratic evolution of nations toward self-government and independence, the State of Vietnam and the kingdoms of Laos and Cambodia could not receive U.S. military assistance as long as they were ruled by France. Not until February 1950, after the French parliament had ratified agreements granting a degree of autonomy to the Associated States of Indochina (Vietnam, Laos, and Cambodia) within the French Union, could the U.S. government recognize these states and respond to French and Vietnamese requests for military and economic aid.

MAAG, Indochina: The Forerunner

On 8 May 1950 Secretary of State Dean G. Acheson concluded consultations with the French government in Paris and announced that the situation in Southeast Asia warranted both economic aid and military equipment for the Associated States of Indochina and for France. To supervise the flow of military assistance, Secretary of Defense George C. Marshall approved the establishment of a small military assistance advisory group. Total authorized strength at the time of its activation was 128 men. The first members of the group arrived in Saigon on 3 August 1950. After the necessary organizational tasks were completed, a provisional detachment— Military Assistance Advisory Group (MAAG), Indochina—was organized on 17 September and assembled in the Saigon-Cholon area on 20 November 1950. The original structure, though temporary, provided for service representation by setting up Army, Navy, and Air Force sections within the group.

Military aid agreements between the United States and the governments of Vietnam, Laos, Cambodia, and France were signed in Saigon on 23 December 1950. Known as the Pentalateral Agreements, these accords formed the basis of U.S. economic and military support. U.S. military assistance was administered by the newly constituted Military Assistance Advisory Group, Indochina. Its first chief was Brigadier General Francis G. Brink, who had assumed command on 10 October 1950. General Brink's main responsibility was to manage the U.S. military assistance program for Vietnam, Cambodia, and Laos and to provide logistical support for the French Union forces. Military training of Vietnamese units remained in the hands of the French Expeditionary Corps, and personnel of the U.S. advisory group had little, if any, influence and no authority in this matter. Because of this restriction, the chief function of the Military Assistance Advisory Group during the early years of U.S. commitment in Indochina was to make sure that equipment supplied by the United States reached its prescribed destination and that it was properly maintained by French Union forces.

On 31 July 1952 General Brink was succeeded as chief of the advisory group by Major General Thomas J. H. Trapnell, who held this position for almost two years. The U.S. chain of command during 1950–1954 ran from the President, as Commander in Chief,

GENERAL BRINK   GENERAL TRAPNELL

to the Department of the Navy (acting as executive agency), to the Commander in Chief, Pacific, and then to the chief of the Military Assistance Advisory Group in Indochina. Early in this period, the chiefs of the advisory groups dealt mainly with the Commander in Chief, Pacific, but when the war began to go badly for the French, higher authorities in Washington, including the President, took a more immediate interest. Increasingly, Washington became concerned about the effectiveness of U.S. military aid to the French Union forces, the expansion of the Vietnamese National Army, and the conduct of the war.

To assess the value and effectiveness of U.S. military aid and to try to exert influence in at least some proportion to the growing U.S. commitment, Admiral Arthur W. Radford, Commander in Chief, Pacific, sent Lieutenant General John W. O'Daniel, Commanding General, U.S. Army, Pacific, on three trips to Indochina. General O'Daniel's visits were made after General Jean de Lattre de Tassigny had been replaced by General Raoul Salan on 1 April 1952, and after General Henri-Eugène Navarre had succeeded General Salan in May of the following year. General O'Daniel's efforts to observe the activities of the French command were only moderately successful. In no way was he able to influence either plans or operations.

General Navarre realized from the beginning that the French Union forces were overextended and tied to defensive positions. He therefore developed a military plan, subsequently named after him, that called for expanding the Vietnamese National Army and assigning it the defensive missions, thus releasing French forces for mobile operations. General Navarre also intended to form more light mobile battalions, and he expected reinforcements from France. With additional U.S. arms and equipment for his forces, Navarre planned to hold the Red River Delta and Cochinchina while building up his mobile reserves. By avoiding decisive battles during the dry season from October 1953 to April 1954, Navarre hoped to assemble his mobile strike forces for an offensive that by 1955 would result in a draw at least. The military plan had a pacification counterpart that would secure the areas under Viet Minh influence.

His plans were unsuccessful, however, despite increased U.S. shipments of arms and equipment. The French politely but firmly prevented American advisers and General O'Daniel from intervening in what they considered their own business. Following instructions from Paris to block the Communist advance into Laos, General Navarre in November 1953 decided to occupy and defend Dien Bien Phu. This fatal decision was based on grave miscalculations, and the Viet Minh overran Dien Bien Phu on 8 May 1954. Their tactical victory marked the end of effective French military operations in the first Indochina War, although fighting continued until 20 July, the date the Geneva Accords were signed.

The Geneva Accords

The Geneva Accords of 20 July 1954 officially ended the fighting in Indochina. As a condition for its participation in the Geneva conference, the United States stipulated that an armistice agreement must at least preserve the southern half of Vietnam. This prerequisite was fulfilled by dividing Vietnam at the 17th parallel. The Geneva agreement also gave independence to Laos and Cambodia. Neither the United States nor the government of South Vietnam formally acknowledged the Geneva Accords, but in a separate, unilateral declaration the United States agreed to adhere to the terms of the agreements.

Some of the provisions contained in articles of the Geneva agreements were to have unforeseen and lasting effects on the organization and application of U.S. military assistance and on the developing command and control arrangements of the U.S. Military Assistance Advisory Group. Among these provisions was Article 16, which prohibited the introduction into Vietnam of troops and other military personnel that had not been in the country at the time of the cease-fire. The provision also fixed the number of advisers in the military assistance group at 888, the total number of

French and Americans in the country on the armistice date. Of the total, the French representation consisted of 262 advisers with the military assistance group and 284 with the Vietnamese Navy and Air Force. Of the 342 Americans only 128 were advisers, as originally authorized before the cease-fire. The remaining spaces were filled on an emergency basis, temporarily with fifteen officers, newly assigned, and almost two hundred Air Force technicians. These technicians were in Vietnam because they had accompanied forty aircraft given to the French early in 1954. Even though the U.S. advisory role in Vietnam was about to change drastically, the magic figure of 342 was on the board and would be difficult to alter.

Articles 17–19 contained restrictions regarding weapons, equipment, ammunition, bases, and military alliances. Shipment of new types of arms, ammunition, and materiel was forbidden. Only on a piece-by-piece basis could worn-out or defective items be replaced, and then only through designated control points. Neither North nor South Vietnam was to establish new military bases, nor could any foreign power exercise control over a military base in Vietnam. Furthermore, neither the North nor the South was to enter into any military alliance or allow itself to be used as an instrument for the resumption of hostilities.

To ensure compliance with these and other provisions of the Geneva agreements, International Control Commissions were set up for Vietnam, Cambodia, and Laos. Each commission consisted of representatives from India, Canada, and Poland, their staffs, and inspection teams. The strength of the International Control Commission in Vietnam—about 670 members—indicated its very considerable inspection and control capability. Because of the terms of the Geneva agreements, the commission's operations tended to favor North Vietnam, while restricting the functions of the Military Assistance Advisory Group and increasing its work load. The U.S. objective of creating a national army and achieving an effective military status for South Vietnam thus was severely handicapped. On the other hand, however, as late as 1959, the International Control Commission was praised by the chief of the U.S. advisory group in 1959 as benefiting South Vietnam and operating as a possible deterrent to Viet Cong attack. South Vietnam thus gained valuable time, which allowed for political consolidation, economic development, and progress toward the establishment of a balanced military force.

Post-Geneva Arrangements

The agony of Dien Bien Phu and the rapidly declining fortunes of the French forces fighting in Vietnam placed Washington in a dilemma. The French request for U.S. armed intervention sharply divided President Dwight D. Eisenhower's advisers. The President decided that U.S. intervention could become a reality only if undertaken with the help of U.S. allies, with the approval of the Congress, and with independence for the Associated States of Indochina. None of these prerequisites was met. During the deliberations on the U.S. course of action, the President consulted with General O'Daniel and subsequently persuaded him to postpone his retirement and accept the assignment as chief of the Military

GENERAL O'DANIEL

Assistance Advisory Group in Indochina. In deference to French sensibilities and to ensure the seniority of the French Commander in Chief in Indochina, O'Daniel relinquished his third star and reverted to the rank of major general.

On 12 April 1954 General O'Daniel replaced General Trapnell and became the third U.S. Army officer to head the advisory group. He brought with him another expert on Indochina, Lieutenant Colonel William B. Rosson. Within two months General O'Daniel obtained French agreement on U.S. participation in training the Vietnamese armed forces. French collaboration with U.S. elements was prodded by the French defeats on the battlefield and the replacement of General Navarre by General Paul Ely. General Ely as High Commissioner for Vietnam and Commander in Chief, French Expeditionary Corps, combined the civil and military authority still exercised by France.

The understanding on U.S. training assistance—the Ely-O'Daniel agreement—had been reached informally on 15 June 1954. It was 3 December, however, before diplomatic clearance allowed the formation of a nucleus of the Franco-American Mission to the Armed Forces of Vietnam. President Eisenhower's special envoy to Saigon, General J. Lawton Collins, concluded a formal agreement with General Ely on 13 December. This agreement provided for the autonomy of the Armed Forces of the State of Vietnam by 1 July 1955 and gave the chief of the U.S. advisory group in Indochina the authority to assist the government of Vietnam in organizing and training its armed forces, beginning 1 January 1955. The agreement also ensured over-all French control of military operations in Indochina.

The Ely-Collins agreement fundamentally changed the U.S. assistance role in Indochina from one of materiel supply and delivery to a true military assistance and advisory role in support of Vietnamese government. With this step, the United States for the first time became fully involved in the future of South Vietnam. The new situation called for a basic reorganization of the advisory group to meet its enlarged responsibilities. In close collaboration with the French, General O'Daniel organized the Training Relations and Instruction Mission (TRIM) on 1 February 1955. The U.S. Military Assistance Advisory Group, in a combined effort with the South Vietnamese and the French, was operating on three levels. Policy was established on the highest level by a committee consisting of the Vietnamese Minister of Defense, a senior French general, and the chief of the U.S. advisory group; a co-ordinating committee on the Defense Ministry level was composed of the same French and U.S. representatives and the Chief of Staff of the Vietnamese armed forces; and, in the field, heads of training teams were attached to Vietnamese units.

These combined arrangements for training the Vietnamese Army continued for fourteen months until the French High Command in Indochina was deactivated on 28 April 1956. On the following day, personnel from the Training Relations and Instruction Mission were reassigned to MAAG's Combat Arms Training and Organization Division. For another year, the French continued to provide advisers to the Vietnamese Navy and Air Force. During its existence, the training mission had 217 spaces for U.S. military personnel, almost two-thirds of the 342 spaces authorized for the entire advisory group. The proportionately high commitment to training activities was undertaken even though it reduced MAAG's ability to deal adequately with growing logistical problems. From the beginning of its operations, most difficulties encountered by the advisory group could be attributed to the shortage of personnel, which in turn stemmed from the ceiling imposed by the Geneva agreements.

In the meantime, the United States decided to decentralize MAAG operations, thus dividing command and administrative burdens and strengthening the U.S. advisory efforts in Indochina. A reorganization of the Military Assistance Advisory Group was also needed to adjust to significant political developments in the area. On 16 May 1955 the United States and Cambodia signed an agreement for direct military aid—a move followed on 25 September by Cambodia's declaring itself a free and independent state. On 20 July, Vietnam announced that it would not participate in talks for the reunification of North and South Vietnam through the elections that were scheduled for the following year, according to the Geneva agreements. On 26 October Premier Ngo Dinh Diem proclaimed the Republic of Vietnam, after deposing former Emperor and Head of State Bao Dai through a national referendum. Diem also became the supreme commander of South Vietnam's armed forces. Meanwhile, in Laos, a coalition government was being negotiated that would include the Communist Pathet Lao group. (An accord was finally reached on 5 August 1956.) In the midst of these events, the last French High Commissioner left Saigon on 16 August 1955. Because of these developments, a reorganization of U.S. military assistance to the newly independent states of Vietnam, Cambodia, and Laos was needed. Consequently, on 13 June 1955 the Military Assistance Advisory Group, Cambodia, was organized in Phnom Penh. Assistance operations in Cambodia and Laos had differed significantly from those in South Vietnam, because activities in Cambodia and Laos had been limited to logistical support. Therefore, the mission of the newly formed advisory group in Cambodia was primarily logistical, in contrast to the mission of the one in Saigon, which included advisory and training duties. Until 1 November 1955, when the Military Assistance Advisory Group, Indochina, was redesignated the Military Assistance Advisory Group, Vietnam, General O'Daniel retained the responsibility for the U.S. Navy and Air Force efforts in Cambodia. To comply with the Geneva agreements, U.S. military assistance and advisory activities in Laos were less conspicuous than in the rest of Indochina. In December 1955 the United States established a Programs Evaluation Office in Vietnam, which was in charge of military assistance. The Programs Evaluation Office operated under the Operations Mission of the U.S. Embassy. An overlap of functions existed in assisting the Royal Lao Air Force. The Air Force section of the Military Assistance Advisory Group, Vietnam, continued to control all military aviation matters in and for Laos. Thus by the end of 1955, the advisory group in Vietnam was no longer responsible for military assistance programming and maintenance inspection for Laos and Cambodia. The final separation of MAAG duties for Vietnam, Laos, and Cambodia was accomplished by 26 October 1956.

In spite of its reduced responsibilities, the Military Assistance Advisory Group, Vietnam, was still too busy to carry out all its remaining duties effectively. While the combined training, including good relations and co-operation with French personnel,

GENERAL WILLIAMS

was proceeding satisfactorily, a bottleneck developed in the area of logistics. Logistic problems had started with the withdrawal of the French Expeditionary Corps. Until the pullout, the French had not allowed the Vietnamese to handle logistics. But with the rapid reduction of their forces, the French handed over logistical responsibilities to the Vietnamese Army at a rate far exceeding the army's ability to assume such duties. The Vietnamese had no personnel trained in logistical operations because the French had not provided the special training.

The Military Assistance Advisory Group, Vietnam, meanwhile had other problems, caused by the difficulty in finding, recovering, relocating, and shipping out excess equipment of the Mutual Defense Assistance Program. Not only did General O'Daniel have to struggle with a logistical nightmare, but he was also hard pressed for personnel in his training mission, because the French were reducing their contingent of advisers. By 18 November 1955, the day General O'Daniel left Vietnam, the French contingent in the training mission had decreased to fifty-eight men.

Lieutenant General Samuel T. Williams was General O'Daniel's successor. One of General Williams' first tasks was to obtain additional personnel to compensate for the reduction of the French element and to handle his mounting logistical requirements. General Williams' plea for more men was supported by the Commander in Chief, Pacific, but Washington was harder to convince. Interpreting Article 16 of the Geneva Accords narrowly, Washington authorities were reluctant to make a move toward any conspicuous increase in the strength of military personnel in South Vietnam. In talks with members of the International Control Commission and the government of South Vietnam, General Williams had ascertained that a one-for-one substitution of U.S. advisers for the departing French would not be considered a violation of the Geneva Accords.

After long and careful deliberation, officials in Washington skirted the issue by maintaining the authorized strength of the Military Assistance Advisory Group, Vietnam, at 342 men. On the other hand, to help General Williams solve his logistical problems, the Temporary Equipment Recovery Mission (TERM) was established on 1 June 1956 with a strength of 350 men. Its primary task was to locate, catalog, ship out, and rebuild excess U.S. military equipment. In addition, the recovery mission was to assist the Vietnamese in training their armed forces, with a view to establishing their own workable logistical support system. Although the activity was subordinate to the MAAG chief in Vietnam, it was not a part of the Military Assistance Advisory Group. (*Chart 1*)

For the next four years, General Williams tried to have the strength of the advisory group raised to 888, the total number of U.S. and French advisers in Vietnam at the time of the armistice. Since the work load of the Temporary Equipment Recovery Mission was decreasing, the logical step was to integrate TERM personnel into the Military Assistance Advisory Group, Vietnam. General Williams believed that raising the strength of the advisory group by merging the two activities would not violate the intent or letter of the Geneva Accords. In April 1960 he reported that the International Control Commission had favorably considered the request to increase MAAG's strength from 342 to 685 spaces, 7 spaces less than the combined totals of the two activities but still over 200 men short of the July 1954 figure. On 5 May 1960 the U.S. government announced that, at the request of the government of South Vietnam, the proposed increase would be authorized. During the following months TERM personnel were integrated into the Military Assistance Advisory Group, Vietnam, which was itself reorganized. (*Charts 2 and 3*)

Response to Insurgency

After the armistice in the summer of 1954 the United States was chiefly concerned with the possibility of overt aggression from North Vietnam. To meet this potential external threat to the developing state of South Vietnam, the United States had formed the Southeast Asia Treaty Organization (SEATO) and had placed South Vietnam under its protection. Since South Vietnam was prohibited from joining any alliance, SEATO's protective shield represented a strong deterrent to the proclaimed intentions of the North Vietnamese to unify all of Vietnam under Communist rule. This security was especially vital to South Vietnam, because it was just beginning to consolidate and establish the authority of the central government in Saigon.

An essential element in making the consolidation process work was the South Vietnamese Army. The army was no more than a

CHART 1—TEMPORARY EQUIPMENT RECOVERY MISSION, 1956

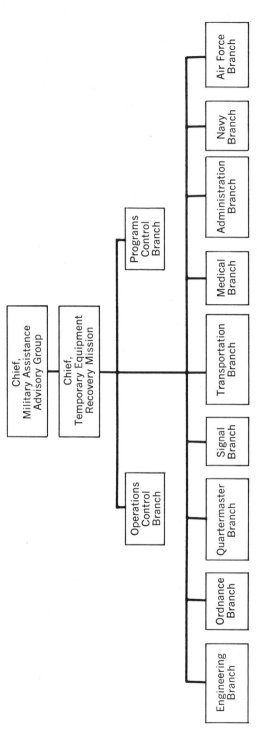

Source: Letter, HQ MAAG, Vietnam, dated 18 August 1956, subject: *Brief Summary of Past Significant Events.*

CHART 2—MILITARY ASSISTANCE ADVISORY GROUP, VIETNAM, 1956

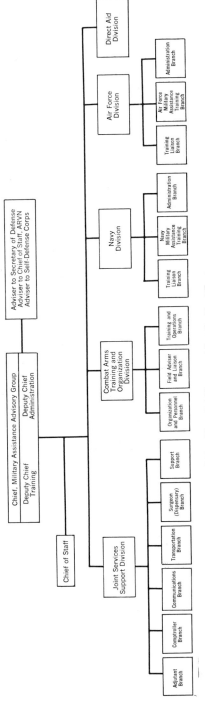

Source: Letter, HQ MAAG, Vietnam, dated 18 August 1956, subject: *Brief Summary of Past Significant Events.*

CHART 3—TEMPORARY EQUIPMENT RECOVERY MISSION, 1960

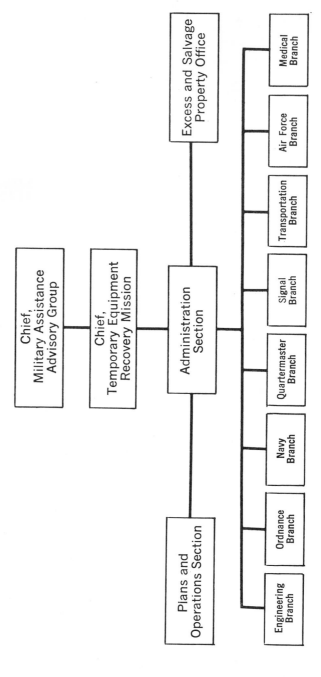

Chief,
Military Assistance
Advisory Group

Chief,
Temporary Equipment
Recovery Mission

Plans and
Operations Section

Administration
Section

Excess and Salvage
Property Office

Engineering
Branch

Ordnance
Branch

Navy
Branch

Quartermaster
Branch

Signal
Branch

Transportation
Branch

Air Force
Branch

Medical
Branch

Source: Study on Army Aspects of the Military Assistance Program in Vietnam (Ft. Leavenworth: HQ, USACGSC, 10 January 1960), p. D–6–1.

concept when the first Indochina War ended. The mission of the Military Assistance Advisory Group was to make this concept a reality. The South Vietnamese government depended on the army to provide a pool of administrators in the capital, the provinces, and the districts; to establish internal security; and to defend the country against outside aggression.

The obstacles in the way of achieving a central authority were towering. The army was rife with dissension, disloyalty, and corruption. Religious sects, such as the Hoa Hao and Cao Dai, and a gangster organization, the Binh Xuyen, had their own armed forces and were using them in a power struggle. In the Central Highlands, the Montagnards, ethnic tribal groups, refused to acknowledge the central government. In addition, some one million Catholic refugees from North Vietnam were being relocated in the south, upsetting a delicate religious balance. The progress of the Diem government toward stability must therefore be measured against this chaotic background.

By 1957 what few had expected to see in South Vietnam— political stability—had been accomplished. The economy was on a sound basis and improving. The armed forces had defeated the dissidents. The achievement obliterated Communist expectations of a take-over more or less by default. Diem's refusal to allow a referendum in 1956 apparently had deprived the North Vietnamese of a legal means by which to gain control of the south.

In 1957 the Communist North Vietnamese Lao Dong Party therefore decided on a change of strategy for winning its objective. The strategy was not new; it was a revival of the Viet Minh insurrection against French domination, and the tactics were those of guerrilla warfare, terror, sabotage, kidnapping, and assassination. The goal was to paralyze the Diem administration by eliminating government officials and severing contact between the countryside and Saigon. At the same time, the Communists would usurp government control, either openly or surreptitiously, depending on the local situation. The new insurgents became known as the Viet Cong, and their political arm was the National Liberation Front, proclaimed in December 1960.

The first, faint signs of a change in Communist strategy, from the plan to take over South Vietnam through political means supported by external pressure to a policy of subversion and insurgency within the country, began to be noticed in 1957. The following year, the Viet Cong intensified and extended their political and guerrilla operations to a point where they created serious problems that threatened South Vietnamese government control in the countryside. Prodded by General Williams and faced with an election,

President Diem belatedly ordered countermeasures in 1959 and committed more forces to internal security. But after the elections, in the fall of 1959, the Viet Cong began to gain the upper hand. Government control was eroding, the countryside and the cities were being isolated from one another, and the economy was suffering.

The crisis called for a re-evaluation of the U.S. effort. In March 1960 General Lyman L. Lemnitzer, U.S. Army Chief of Staff, visited South Vietnam. He reported to the Joint Chiefs of Staff that the situation had deteriorated markedly during the past months. President Diem had declared the country to be in a state of all-out war against the Viet Cong and requested increased U.S. assistance in materiel and training. General Lemnitzer supported the request and recommended that the training and organization of the Vietnamese Army should be modified to shift the emphasis from conventional to antiguerrilla warfare training. He offered U.S. Army personnel, in the form of mobile training teams, to help achieve this objective. In April the Commander in Chief, Pacific, recommended that a co-ordinated plan be developed for the over-all U.S. effort in support of the government of South Vietnam. The Departments of State and Defense sanctioned this recommendation.

In Saigon the U.S. Ambassador, the chief of the advisory group, and other senior officials, constituting what was known as the Country Team, drew up a planning document that dealt with the political, military, economic, and psychological requirements for fighting the Communist insurgency. This Counterinsurgency Plan for South Vietnam contained significant reforms, many of which had been proposed to the government of South Vietnam for some time but had not been accepted. Among the prominent features of the Counterinsurgency Plan were the reorganization of the South Vietnamese command and control organization; an increase in Vietnam's armed forces from 150,000 to 170,000 men; and additional funds of about $49 million to support the plan. The Counterinsurgency Plan urged the Vietnamese to streamline their command structure to allow for central direction, to eliminate overlapping functions, and to pool military, paramilitary, and civilian resources.

The Military Assistance Advisory Group was also eager to provide more advisers at lower levels of command. At the beginning of the U.S. training effort, advisers had been limited to higher commands down to the division level, and to schools, training centers, territorial headquarters, and logistic installations. Only on a very small scale and on a temporary basis had U.S. advisers been attached to battalion-size units. The new emphasis on counterinsurgency training early in 1960 changed this situation. In May 1960, coinciding with the integration of TERM personnel into the advisory group, the MAAG chief was authorized to increase the number of personnel assignments to field advisory duties at battalion levels. These assignments remained temporary, however, and were still made selectively—mainly to armored, artillery, and marine battalions. Toward the end of 1960, the government of Vietnam transferred the paramilitary forces of its Civil Guard and Self Defense Corps from the Interior Ministry to the Ministry of Defense. Both organizations, vital to the

GENERAL McGARR. (*Photograph taken before his promotion to lieutenant general.*)

maintenance of security in the provinces and districts, thus became eligible for MAAG training and assistance. In addition, U.S. Special Forces teams began training the newly established, 5,000-man, Vietnamese Ranger force by the end of 1960. Clearly, the U.S. commitment in Vietnam was growing. At this time, General Williams ended his almost five-year tour as MAAG chief. He was succeeded by Lieutenant General Lionel C. McGarr on 1 September 1960.

In Washington the Eisenhower administration was replaced by the Kennedy administration. Among President John F. Kennedy's first concerns was the situation in Vietnam. At this crucial time, the Country Team's proposals for countering the Viet Cong insurgency arrived in Washington. Subsequently, the President decided to continue U.S. support for South Vietnam and increased both funds and personnel in support of the Diem government. On 3 April 1961 the United States and South Vietnam signed the Treaty of Amity and Economic Relations in Saigon. One week later President Diem won re-election in his country by an overwhelming majority. To strengthen U.S.-Vietnamese ties further, President Kennedy sent Vice President Lyndon B. Johnson to Saigon on 11 May. In a joint communiqué issued two days later, the United States announced it would grant additional U.S. military and economic aid to South Vietnam in its fight against Communist forces.

These measures, taken by President Kennedy, were based on

preliminary surveys and consultations and on the recommendations of a temporary organization set up to deal with the crisis. In January 1961 the Secretary of Defense, Thomas S. Gates, Jr., had dispatched Major General Edward G. Lansdale to Vietnam. On the general's return, the Deputy Secretary of Defense, Roswell L. Gilpatric, was put in charge of an interdepartmental task force, subsequently known as Task Force, Vietnam, which identified and defined the actions the new administration was about to undertake. In Saigon a counterpart task force was established, its members taken from the Country Team. In addition, General McGarr, the MAAG chief, was brought to Washington in April to give his advice.

Washington had also accepted significant points of the Country Team's Counterinsurgency Plan, including support by the Military Assistance Program for a 20,000-man increase in the Vietnamese armed forces, for a 68,000-man Civil Guard and a 40,000-man Self Defense Corps, and for more U.S. advisers for these additional forces. In May President Kennedy appointed Frederick C. Nolting, Jr., as Ambassador to South Vietnam, replacing Elbridge Durbrow. An economic survey mission, headed by Dr. Eugene Staley of the Stanford Research Institute, visited Vietnam during June and July and submitted its findings to President Kennedy on 29 July 1961. Later, in an address to the Vietnamese National Assembly in October 1961, President Diem referred to Dr. Staley's report, emphasizing the inseparable impact of military and economic assistance on internal security.

Soon after the return of the Staley mission, President Kennedy announced at a press conference on 11 October 1961 that General Maxwell D. Taylor would visit Vietnam to investigate the military situation and would report back to him personally. Dr. Walt W. Rostow, Chairman of the Policy Planning Council, Department of State, accompanied General Taylor. Upon its return, the Taylor-Rostow mission recommended a substantial increase in the U.S. advisory effort; U.S. combat support (mainly tactical airlift); further expansion of the Vietnamese armed forces; and support for the strategic hamlet program, an early attempt at Vietnamization.

Subsequently, the military effort was directed primarily at carrying out these proposals. The task was more than the MAAG headquarters in Vietnam could handle. In November 1961 therefore President Kennedy decided to upgrade the U.S. command by forming the U.S. Military Assistance Command, Vietnam (MACV), and selected General Paul D. Harkins as commander. General Harkins had been serving as Deputy Commanding General, U.S. Army, Pacific, and had been actively involved in the Pacific Com-

MAIN ENTRANCE TO MAAG HEADQUARTERS LOCATED ON DAILO HUNG DAO, *1962.*

mand's contingency planning for Vietnam. Following an interview with President Kennedy in early 1962, he went to Saigon and established Headquarters, Military Assistance Command, Vietnam, on 8 February 1962.

Command Relationships

From 7 November 1950 through 7 February 1962 a single headquarters provided command and control for the U.S. military effort in Vietnam. The number of authorized spaces increased from the original 128 in 1950 to 2,394 by early 1962.

The responsibility for directing and controlling military assistance programs lay with both the legislative and executive branches of the U.S. government. The Mutual Defense Assistance Act of 1949 provided the basis for these programs in Vietnam. Within the executive branch, major assistance duties were performed by the Office of the President, the Department of Defense, and the Department of State. Policies and objectives of military assistance to Vietnam from 1950 to 1962 were based on decisions made by three different administration.

In the Department of Defense the Joint Chiefs of Staff determined the military objectives. The Assistant Secretary of Defense for International Security Affairs co-ordinated the broad political and military guidelines established by the White House and the Departments of State and Defense. The Commander in Chief, Pacific, provided specific guidance and direction to Headquarters, Military Assistance Advisory Group, Vietnam.

As the President's personal representative, the U.S. Ambassador to South Vietnam was charged with over-all responsibility for the co-ordination and supervision of U.S. activities in Vietnam. On political and economic matters, he was guided by the Department of State. The chief of the Military Assistance Advisory Group in Vietnam was responsible to the ambassador for military matters under the Mutual Security Program and, as senior military adviser, was a member of the Country Team.

CHAPTER II

The Military Assistance Command, Vietnam: February 1962–July 1965

The question of establishing a unified military command in South Vietnam was first raised in October 1961. After President Kennedy had bolstered the U.S. commitment in May and again in October, in terms of both personnel and funds, the Military Assistance Advisory Group reorganized to meet the increased demand for field advisers to the South Vietnamese armed forces. General Taylor's mission to Vietnam in October revealed that these measures were inadequate for dealing with the Communist insurgency; therefore, in mid-November the President decided that the United States would assume a growing operational support role in addition to the existing advisory, training, and logistical missions. This decision marked the beginning of a new phase in U.S. support of the South Vietnamese government and its armed forces.

Consequently, the U.S. command structure in Vietnam, which had become overextended even before the new requirements had been established in the President's program, had to be reorganized. In mid-November Secretary of Defense Robert S. McNamara charged the Joint Chiefs of Staff with this task. The new command was to be named the U.S. Military Assistance Command, Vietnam (USMACV).

At the time, the Military Assistance Advisory Group was the only U.S. military headquarters in South Vietnam. A joint organization, it contained an Army, Navy, and Air Force section, each responsible for advising its counterpart in the Vietnamese armed forces and for assisting the chief of the advisory group in administering the Military Assistance Program. Logistical and administrative support of the Military Assistance Advisory Group was provided through service channels. The chief of the advisory group, General McGarr, however, exercised operational control over all U.S. Army units. For their logistical support, however, the units depended on Lieutenant General Paul W. Caraway, Commanding General, U.S. Army, Ryukyu Islands (USARYIS), on Okinawa.

When the first U.S. Army aviation units arrived in Vietnam in December 1961, the need for logistical support sharply increased. Since no U.S. Army element in South Vietnam could provide the support, General James F. Collins, Commander in Chief, U.S. Army, Pacific, directed the 9th Logistic Command on Okinawa to send a logistic support team to South Vietnam to set up a supply service between the newly arrived aviation units and U.S. Army, Ryukyu Islands. On 17 December 1961 an eleven-man team from the 9th. Logistic Command arrived in Vietnam. As the support requirements increased, the team was expanded to 323 men and designated USARYIS Support Group (Provisional). This group formed the nucleus that eventually became the headquarters of U.S. Army, Vietnam—the Army component of the U.S. Military Assistance Command, Vietnam.

Meantime, plans for the establishment of the U.S. Military Assistance Command, Vietnam, had gone forward at command headquarters directly concerned with this matter. Planners generally agreed that the Commander, U.S. Military Assistance Command, Vietnam, should have full responsibility for and authority over all U.S. military activities and operations in Vietnam. However, regarding the application of this principle, the degree of authority, and the place within the chain of command, the planners took different approaches. The key problem, in retrospect, was just where to find the slot for this new unified command and who would be in immediate control.

The Joint Chiefs of Staff proposed forming a unified command that would report directly to them. The commander would control all U.S. forces in South Vietnam employed in a combined effort against the Viet Cong; he would also be the principal U.S. military adviser and sole spokesman for American military affairs in Vietnam. Additional responsibilities would include U.S. intelligence operations, economic aid relating to counterinsurgency, and any functions of the Military Assistance Advisory Group dealing with improvement of the combat effectiveness of the Vietnamese armed forces. The chief of the Military Assistance Advisory Group would retain control of the training mission and would continue to represent the Commander in Chief, Pacific, in planning and administering the Military Assistance Program. General Collins, Commander in Chief, U.S. Army, Pacific, agreed with the proposals of the Joint Chiefs but recommended in addition that all activities of the Military Assistance Advisory Group come directly under the unified commander in Vietnam.

Admiral Harry D. Felt, Commander in Chief, Pacific, raised objections to the Joint Chiefs' proposal of assigning the U.S. Military

Assistance Command, Vietnam, directly to the Joint Chiefs. In Admiral Felt's view, the Communists were threatening all of Southeast Asia, not just South Vietnam; therefore, a single military effort, co-ordinated by the Commander in Chief, Pacific, was required. Accordingly, he suggested forming a subordinate unified command in Vietnam under the Pacific Command. The Department of State concurred with Admiral Felt's proposal provided the U.S. Ambassador to South Vietnam would retain over-all authority of U.S. activities in the country.

Deliberations on the structure of the U.S. Military Assistance Command, Vietnam, and the headquarters' position in the chain of command were complicated by existing contingency plans. Separate sets of plans had been drawn up for possible U.S. unilateral operations on the mainland of Southeast Asia and for combined operations of the Southeast Asia Treaty Organization (SEATO) as well. A joint or combined headquarters was provided for in these plans, which was to be headed by the Deputy Commander in Chief, U.S. Army, Pacific, General Harkins. According to these contingency plans, General Harkins' headquarters was to be under the control of Admiral Felt as Commander in Chief, Pacific.

Because the joint (or combined) field commander in most contingency plans would be the Deputy Commander in Chief, U.S. Army, Pacific, the headquarters of the U.S. Army, Pacific, had prepared many of these plans and also was to provide the nucleus for the designated operational staffs. For this reason Admiral Felt had decided that the field commander would exercise control of the ground forces as his own Army component commander. This decision was consistent with Army and joint doctrine regarding joint task forces. It followed that this doctrinal precedent would be applied in establishing the U.S. Military Assistance Command, Vietnam. The precedent did not apply to the Air Force and Navy components and their commanders, however, which were to be provided by the Pacific Air Force and Navy commands. The reason was the comparatively small effort required by these two services.

The Command Is Established

With the approval of President Kennedy and Secretary of Defense McNamara and by direction of the Joint Chiefs of Staff, Admiral Felt established the U.S. Military Assistance Command, Vietnam, on 8 February 1962, as a subordinate unified command under his control. Lieutenant General Paul D. Harkins, the Deputy Commander in Chief, U.S. Army, Pacific, who, as the commander-

GENERAL HARKINS

designate for the task force headquarters in the event of operations in Southeast Asia, had participated in the planning for such operations, was appointed Commander, U.S. Military Assistance Command, Vietnam, and promoted to general.

In his new position, General Harkins was the senior U.S. military commander in the Republic of Vietnam and, as such, responsible for U.S. military policy, operations, and assistance there. General Harkins had the task of advising the Vietnamese government on security, organization, and employment of their military and paramilitary forces. As provided for in the organization of the task force headquarters in the contingency plans, MACV's commander was also his own Army component commander.

With an initial authorized strength of 216 men (113 Army), the Military Assistance Command was envisaged as a temporary headquarters that would be withdrawn once the Viet Cong insurgency was brought under control. In that event, the Military Assistance Advisory Group would be restored to its former position as the principal U.S. headquarters in South Vietnam. For this reason, the advisory group was retained as a separate headquarters under Major General Charles J. Timmes, who had succeeded General McGarr. The advisory group was responsible to the Military Assistance Command for advisory and operational matters and to the Commander in Chief, Pacific, for the administration of the Military Assistance Program. Although general logistic support continued on an individual service basis, the Military Assistance Command was supported by the Headquarters, Support Activity, Saigon, a small Navy logistical operation.

The temporary character of the new MACV headquarters was further emphasized by the decision initially to limit General Harkins' planning tasks to Vietnam. General Harkins' responsibilities, however, soon expanded when he was assigned broader planning duties connected with U.S. unilateral and SEATO contingencies. Admiral Felt directed General Harkins to prepare the support of the Pacific

Command's plan of action in the event of insurgency and overt aggression in Southeast Asia. In addition, General Harkins was to draft other plans in support of SEATO, thus shifting planning responsibilities in some areas from U.S. Army, Pacific, to the Military Assistance Command. This was a logical trend because General Harkins was still the commander-designate of joint and combined SEATO forces. Before the year was out, such contingency responsibilities were to contribute to a reappraisal of the need and desirability of a separate Army component command under General Harkins' headquarters.

After the Military Assistance Command had been established, the Pacific Air Forces formed the 2d Advance Squadron in Vietnam. The squadron originally functioned as the air component command and later evolved into the air component command headquarters in Vietnam. No immediate steps were taken to establish a naval component command on the Southeast Asia mainland, because one was not needed at the time. Naval duties were handled by the Navy section of the Military Assistance Advisory Group and by Headquarters, Support Activity, Saigon.

As the senior U.S. military commander in Vietnam, General Harkins was directly responsible for all U.S. military policy, operations, and assistance in Vietnam. He was authorized to discuss both U.S. and Vietnamese military operations directly with President Diem and other Vietnamese leaders. General Harkins also advised the Vietnamese on all matters relative to the security, organization, and use of their armed forces and of counterinsurgency or other paramilitary forces. He had direct access to the Pacific commander in chief and through him to the Joint Chiefs of Staff and the Secretary of Defense. Since the U.S. Ambassador was responsible for U.S. political matters and basic policy, General Harkins was to consult him on these subjects; if the two officials disagreed, both were free to submit their respective positions to Washington. The ambassador and the commander were to keep each other fully informed, especially on high-level contacts with the Vietnamese government, on major military plans, and on pending operations.

Command and control of Vietnamese forces remained with Vietnamese commanders, with General Harkins acting as the senior U.S. adviser. The Vietnamese organization provided that the Commander in Chief of the Vietnamese armed forces also be the commander of the Vietnamese Army (ARVN); he was, in every respect, his own Army component commander. Although this arrangement had not been a determining factor in the organization of the Military Assistance Command, the compatibility of the two command structures was to be an important influence when the issue of a separate U.S. Army component commander was raised later.

On 15 May 1962 General Harkins' responsibilities broadened when Admiral Felt established the U.S. Military Assistance Command, Thailand (USMACTHAI), and appointed General Harkins its commander. In this capacity General Harkins had essentially the same latitude and authority as in his position as head of the Military Assistance Command, Vietnam. The Thailand command initially consisted of the following groups: the men and equipment of a U.S. joint task force in Thailand, originally deployed as an element of a SEATO exercise and later held there because of Communist activity in Laos; the Joint U.S. Military Assistance Group, Thailand; and other U.S. military elements deployed to Thailand. Later in 1962, Major General Theodore J. Conway, Chief, Joint U.S. Military Assistance Group, Thailand, was designated to serve concurrently as General Harkins' deputy in Thailand. A staff was formed to assist General Conway with these additional duties. Administrative support of units and elements in Thailand remained the responsibility of the separate services. Thus, while directing U.S. military activities in Vietnam, General Harkins also took charge in Thailand of the Military Assistance Program, the planning and support of Army activities, and contingency plans and exercises.

The Military Assistance Advisory Group

During the conferences that led to the establishment of the Military Assistance Command, Vietnam, the question of how to fit the existing Military Assistance Advisory Group (MAAG) into the new command structure was discussed. The planners, concerned about this problem, were aware that the Military Assistance Command, at least temporarily, would replace the advisory group as the principal U.S. military headquarters in Vietnam and would also absorb other functions that the advisory group had been charged with in the past. In retaining both headquarters, a certain amount of duplication would be unavoidable. Although abolishing the advisory group as a separate organization would have avoided this duplication, MAAG's traditional role and its working relationship with the Vietnamese armed forces, established over a ten-year period, would have been sacrificed, together with MAAG's institutional expertise, which the new command had yet to acquire.

For these reasons, the Military Assistance Advisory Group was retained. The MAAG chief, General Timmes, continued to exercise control over U.S. Army units. He also was charged with the development and administration of the Military Assistance Program and the day-to-day advisory and training effort for the Vietnamese armed forces.

The U.S. Army's chain of command arrangements were not changed by the establishment of the Military Assistance Command in Vietnam. The Commander in Chief, U.S. Army, Pacific, General Collins, continued to provide administrative and logistical support to U.S. Army units in Vietnam through Headquarters, U.S. Army, Ryukyu Islands. General Harkins had operational control of Army units, but he delegated the authority to General Timmes. Thus, even though functions of the Military Assistance Command and the advisory group technically overlapped, the duplication in some areas of responsibility did not interfere with U.S. assistance and advisory activities in Vietnam.

U.S. Army Support Group, Vietnam

In March 1962 Headquarters, U.S. Army, Pacific, issued a letter of instruction that removed the "provisional" designation from the U.S. Army Support Group, Vietnam, attached it to U.S. Army, Ryukyu Islands, for administrative and logistical support, and made its commanding officer the deputy Army component commander under the Military Assistance Command. In turn, all U.S. Army units in Vietnam (excluding advisory attachments) were assigned to the Army Support Group for administrative and logistical needs. Although the support group was under the operational control of the Military Assistance Command, it was also required to support U.S. Army, Pacific, in carrying out its missions. In effect, this arrangement removed the support group from the command of U.S. Army, Ryukyu Islands, even though the group continued to depend on U.S. Army, Ryukyu Islands, for logistical and administrative support. The twofold mission of the group was to support combat operations and to provide the nucleus for a type-B logistical command headquarters that would direct combat support units in Vietnam under existing contingency plans.

In July 1962 the Commander in Chief, U.S. Army, Pacific, General Collins, corrected the dual arrangement by permanently assigning the U.S. Army Support Group, Vietnam, to U.S. Army, Ryukyu Islands. (*Chart 4*) This command relationship was to continue, until 1965, when the successor to the group, U.S. Army,

CHART 4—U.S. COMMAND RELATIONSHIPS IN VIETNAM, 1962

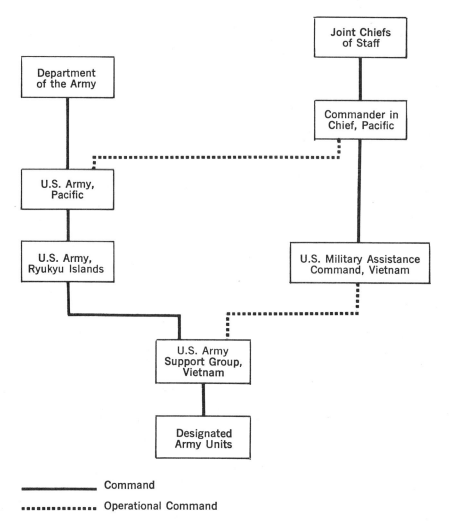

Command
Operational Command

Source: Department of Army Management Review Team, Review and Analysis of the Army Command and Control Structure in Vietnam, Vol. II (Washington: 29 July 1968), p. AV–12.

Vietnam, was placed directly under U.S. Army, Pacific, thereby eliminating the Ryukyu Islands headquarters from the chain of command. Throughout the entire period, the support group remained under the operational control of the Military Assistance Command. The commander of the support group, although still the deputy Army component commander of the Military Assistance Command in Vietnam, became responsible for executing the plans and directives of General Caraway in the Ryukyus as well as for carrying out General Collins' missions in South Vietnam. Operational control of most Army units, particularly aviation companies, rested with General Timmes, chief of the advisory group in Vietnam, to whom General Harkins had delegated this authority. Under this arrangement, Army strength rose from 948 to 7,885 men during 1962.

Control of Army aviation assets at this time illustrates the multiple lines of responsibility in Vietnam. Since General Timmes had operational control of Army aviation units, the senior adviser assigned to a Vietnamese Army corps could directly request U.S. Army aviation support. For example, the Vietnamese corps commander could initiate and plan a helicopter operation. The adviser assigned to the corps would formally transmit a request to the commanding officer of a U.S. Army helicopter company for execution. Actual planning for such an operation thus involved the Vietnamese corps commander and his staff, the Military Assistance Advisory Group's representative, and the commander of the helicopter company. Issues which could not be resolved locally between the adviser and the commanding officer of the helicopter unit were referred to General Harkins through appropriate channels. Army aviation unit commanders, therefore, had to deal with and satisfy, on a daily basis, the Vietnamese Army, the Military Assistance Advisory Group, the Military Assistance Command, and the U.S. Army Support Group. The support group, in turn, had to carry out responsibilities to the U.S. Army, Pacific; U.S. Army, Ryukyu Islands; and the Military Assistance Command in Vietnam.

Contingency Considerations

Concern over the conflicting command and control arrangements established by the various contingency plans resulted in a series of conferences in the fall of 1962 to examine the situation and, in particular, to study the need for a separate Army component commander. The responsibilities assigned to General Harkins under various contingency situations prompted him to recommend alternate command arrangements for Vietnam. His recommendation led to counterproposals by the Joint Chiefs of Staff, Admiral Felt, and the service components. Strongly influenced by the Laotian crisis in 1962, General Harkins proposed that a ground component command headquarters, separate from the joint or combined higher headquarters, be established for all unilateral and SEATO contingency plans for operations in Southeast Asia. If these plans for Vietnam, Thailand, or Laos were to be implemented, a combat-capable Army component commander and staff should be available to conduct the land war. Although the U.S. Army Support Group was the Army component command within the Military Assistance Command at the time, its functions were limited to logistical and administrative matters and excluded operational matters, which were the concern of the chief of the Military Assistance Advisory Group. Neither headquarters could qualify as a true Army ground component command.

In commenting on General Harkins' proposal, General Collins indicated that a headquarters like the Army corps headquarters provided in contingency plans would be appropriate for the conduct of ground operations. The corps headquarters would also be able to perform the other duties of a ground component command under joint (Military Assistance Command) or combined (SEATO) direction, at least during the first stages of an operation. General Collins emphasized, however, that his proposal would be valid only if the joint or combined commander was a U.S. Army general officer.

General Harkins' proposal also dealt with the subject of the command structure in Thailand. He suggested that Army units in Thailand be placed directly under the deputy commander of the Military Assistance Command, Thailand, who would then be the Army component commander there. Admiral Felt, however, believed that the operations of the Army component command in Thailand should remain within Army (U.S. Army, Pacific) channels rather than being vested in a joint headquarters; he also indicated that General Harkins should be his own ground component commander. Finally, Admiral Felt recommended new arrangements for Thailand that would relieve General Harkins of all responsibilities in Thailand and Laos.

These issues were considered at a meeting held in Hawaii in October 1962. Secretary of Defense Robert S. McNamara decided that General Harkins should retain his responsibilities in Thailand and his title of Commander, U.S. Military Assistance Command, Thailand (actually, the title decided upon at the meeting was Commander, U.S. Military Assistance Command, Vietnam-Thailand). The chief of the Military Assistance Group in Thailand would be the deputy commander of the Military Assistance Command, Thailand, under General Harkins and would have operational control over all U.S. forces in Thailand. Logistic and administrative support of the forces there would remain the responsibility of the service components of the Pacific Command. A small joint staff of the Military Assistance Command would remain in Thailand, primarily for planning purposes. These arrangements became effective on 30 October 1962.

General Harkins raised other command questions at this conference, some of which were discussed but not settled. He pointed out, for example, that the component commands in Vietnam were neither organized nor staffed to carry out the planning, operational, and administrative tasks normally performed by component commands. In Vietnam the component commanders had had primarily administrative and logistical duties. General Harkins, therefore, suggested that the component headquarters be reorganized and strengthened, so that they could assume their full share of command functions in Vietnam, Thailand, and Laos, if unilateral or SEATO plans were ever implemented.

The most significant result of the discussions about component commands was that the Pacific Air Forces' 2d Advance Squadron, the largest U.S. Air Force headquarters in Southeast Asia outside the Philippines, was expanded and redesignated 2d Air Division. The division controlled most operations of the Pacific Air Forces of the mainland of Southeast Asia. The command channel originated with the Commander in Chief, Pacific, went to the commander of the Military Assistance Command in Vietnam and Thailand, and then to the commanding general of the 2d Air Division; the Pacific Air Forces provided administrative and logistical support. General Harkins thus acquired a responsive Air Force component command. For certain air operations over the Southeast Asia mainland outside the operational area of General Harkins' command, however, the 2d Air Division continued to report to the commander in chief of the Pacific Air Forces, and through him to Admiral Felt. The decision limited General Harkins' authority over, and responsibility for, air operations other than those concerned with direct support and assistance to Vietnamese forces.

Since naval activity in Southeast Asia had not significantly increased, a naval component command was not established.

During 1962 the strength of U.S. military personnel in Vietnam rose from about 1,000 to over 11,000 men. Each service was responsible for its own logistic support, although Headquarters, Support Activity, Saigon, continued to provide logistical and administrative support to General Harkins' headquarters and countrywide support to all advisory personnel, including the Army's. Support for other Army forces in Vietnam came from Okinawa and the continental United States. Logistic operations were thus decentralized with only limited over-all co-ordination; common-user arrangements for major logistic items had not yet been developed.

Deputy Army Component Commander

Realizing that the command and control arrangements governing Army combat service support in Vietnam should be refined, General Collins acted to modify them in March 1963. With the concurrence of the Military Assistance Command and the approval of Admiral Felt, General Collins issued a letter of instruction in August 1963 appointing General Harkins the Army component commander for current operations in Vietnam. In addition, Brigadier General Joseph W. Stilwell, Commanding General, U.S. Army Support Group, Vietnam, was designated deputy Army component commander of the Military Assistance Command, Vietnam. This change had the effect of channeling to General Stilwell most problems peculiar to the Army. General Harkins, as the head of the Military Assistance Command, had operational control over Army units; General Stilwell, as his deputy, exercised command less operational control of the units and continued to provide combat service support.

These changes were minor since, in practice, responsibilities had already been divided along these lines. The new instructions did clarify command relationships between the Military Assistance Command, the advisory group, the support group, and U.S. Army, Ryukyu Islands, concerning control over Army advisers and organizations in Vietnam. Furthermore, the new arrangements were aligned with Admiral Felt's concept of a command structure in Vietnam. Additional advantages included improved control of Army men and equipment needed for counterinsurgency operations, and better co-ordination between the Military Assistance Command and the Vietnamese Army because of the similarity between the two organizations.

The South Vietnamese Joint General Staff, like the Military Assistance Command, had direct operational control over Vietnamese Army forces, while the Vietnamese Army's headquarters exercised command less operational control, performing primarily support and training missions. Under the revised command arrangements, the U.S. Army Support Group was responsible for those component command missions and functions pertaining to Army activities in South Vietnam, particularly combat service support. U.S. Army, Ryukyu Islands, continued to exercise command less operational control over the support group.

In addition to the duties carried over from the previous command structure, the support group became responsible for co-ordinating, through the Military Assistance Command, Vietnamese assistance in providing security for U.S. Army organizations in

Vietnam. The support group also was to provide logistical support for units of the U.S. Army Security Agency in South Vietnam, common supply support to other U.S. armed services in accordance with locally approved interservice support agreements, a base from which to expand U.S. Army activities in Vietnam, and command elements as needed to direct and support additional U.S. Army units arriving in Vietnam. Finally, the support group was to undertake long-range base development planning. It was to advise Army headquarters both in the Ryukyus and in Hawaii of all Army component command functions being delegated to General Stilwell by General Harkins.

Throughout 1963 the duties of the U.S. Army Support Group steadily increased, particularly those pertaining to combat support activities and logistic requirements. During the year, the U.S. buildup continued, especially in aviation, communications, intelligence, special warfare, and logistic units, reaching a total of 17,068 men, of which 10,916 were Army. Because of this expansion, General Stilwell late in 1963 proposed that the name of the support group be changed to U.S. Army Support Command, Vietnam. General Harkins concurred and General Collins and Admiral Felt approved the redesignation, providing the change in no way altered the group's existing or potential roles and missions. The new designation went into effect on 1 March 1964.

Army–Air Force Relations

In October 1962 Admiral Felt assigned General Harkins the task of organizing and directing an airlift system in Southeast Asia. The U.S. Air Force's 315th Air Division in Japan was to exercise flight control over all aircraft in the system and supply a combat cargo group to provide actual airlift. General Harkins placed the cargo group under the 2d Air Division to satisfy the requirement of the Unified Action Armed Forces doctrine, which specified that component commanders retain control of units of their own service.

The requirements of the Unified Action Armed Forces, as well as Admiral Felt's directives, raised command problems between the U.S. Army and Air Force. The problems centered around the functions of the air operations centers in Vietnam and the use of Army Caribou aircraft. The Air Force interpreted the term "air" as embracing all aircraft and wanted all aviation units, including those from the Army, to report to Air Force control facilities. Army commanders held that Army aviation elements should be controlled by the ground commander.

A directive of 18 August 1962 from General Harkins stated that the air operations center, with the Air Force component commander as co-ordinator, was to advise on command decisions and pass them on to all forces concerned. Army commanders felt that this policy was inconsistent with the operational responsibility of the senior U.S. Army adviser to each Vietnamese Army corps and that it violated the principle of unity of command. The Air Force component commander, on the other hand, pointed out that the corps' senior advisers lacked an air operations and planning staff and could not exercise effective control of supporting aviation units. Under these circumstances, the Air Force component was the proper agency to assume air control; Army interests could be served by Army representation at corps air support operations centers. Since Admiral Felt had directed the Air Force component commander to co-ordinate operations of all U.S. aviation units through the tactical air control system, the Army lost direct control of its aviation units.

Reorganization of MACV Headquarters (May 1964)

With the expansion of U.S. military activities in Vietnam, conflicting and overlapping roles of U.S. headquarters in Vietnam—especially of the Military Assistance Advisory Group and the Military Assistance Command—became more apparent. Thus in early 1964 the reorganization of the American command structure again came under high-level review. Various proposals focused primarily on the consolidation of the headquarters of both the advisory group and the Military Assistance Command but touched also on such questions as the component command structure and MACV's continuation as a subordinate unified command.

Consolidation of the two headquarters had been considered when the Military Assistance Command was first activated in February 1962. At that time, it was decided that the command should set the policy and supervise the conduct of the counterinsurgency effort in Vietnam, but not become involved with the details of planning the Military Assistance Program, nor with the day-to-day advisory effort for the Vietnamese armed forces. These routine functions were to remain the responsibility of the advisory group. Moreover, the Military Assistance Command had originally been organized as a temporary headquarters.

Almost from the beginning some duplication of effort between the two headquarters had been unavoidable. Since the advisory group was under MACV's operational control, the command had review authority over the group's activities. Unorthodox command

Main Entrance to MACV I Headquarters Located at 137 Pasture, *1962.*

channels resulted, funding for some activities became complicated, and advisers in the field with Vietnamese units felt they served two masters. As the tactical situation deteriorated, it became more and more difficult to distinguish between the respective missions, functions, and responsibilities of the two headquarters. Vague and overlapping channels also existed in the Vietnamese armed forces and in the government of Vietnam, and the management of military and nonmilitary units available to assist the Vietnamese Army suffered. Finally, duplication also occurred between MACV and MAAG headquarters and the service components, especially in providing logistical and administrative support to advisory detachments in the field.

As early as September 1962 General Harkins proposed that all advisory group functions except those related to the Military Assistance Program be transferred to the component commanders of the Military Assistance Command, and that the headquarters of the advisory group become a staff division of MACV headquarters. This proposal was discussed with the Commander in Chief, Pacific, and the Joint Chiefs of Staff several times during 1962 and 1963.

Admiral Felt opposed the plan primarily because he did not want MACV headquarters to become bogged down in the details of the Military Assistance Program and day-to-day advisory activities.

Following discussions with Secretary McNamara and General Earle G. Wheeler, the Army Chief of Staff, in March 1964 in Vietnam, General Harkins on 12 March submitted a new proposal for consolidating the Military Assistance Command and the advisory group. General Harkins' primary objective was to eliminate the advisory group as an intervening command in the U.S. training and advisory effort, thus enabling the Military Assistance Command to manage U.S. military programs and resources more directly, in conformity with the requirements of the South Vietnamese government's new Chien Thang National Pacification Plan. Noting that 65 percent of the U.S. military effort involved Army personnel or units, and that 95 percent of the counterinsurgency effort by the Vietnamese armed forces was carried out by their army, General Harkins requested operational control over all Army advisory activities. Under his proposed reorganization, MACV headquarters essentially would be a U.S. Army specified command, rather than a subordinate unified command under the Commander in Chief, Pacific. General Harkins wanted to retain a joint staff, although that staff would be heavily weighted with U.S. Army positions. At the same time, General Harkins would be his own Army component commander. All Army administrative and logistical support activities previously handled by the Army section of the Military Assistance Advisory Group would pass to a single headquarters, U.S. Army Support Command, Vietnam, which had shared such responsibilities with the section. With the elimination of the Army section of the advisory group, the Army advisory program would become General Harkins' direct responsibility.

Under General Harkins' proposal, all other advisory activities of the individual services would become subordinate to their respective component commands. U.S. Navy and Marine Corps advisory activities would be handled by the Naval Advisory Group, which for all practical purposes was a redesignation of the Navy section of the Military Assistance Advisory Group. The chief of the Naval Advisory Group would be the Navy component commander of the Military Assistance Command and exercise direct operational control over Navy and Marine Corps advisory detachments. The Commanding General, 2d Air Division, would be MACV's Air Force component commander. The Air Force section of the Military Assistance Advisory Group was to pass to the operational control of the 2d Air Division and become the Air Force Advisory Group, which in turn was to exercise direct operational control over Air Force advisory units. Air Force responsibilities in the Military Assistance Program, however, would be retained by MACV headquarters. These steps would place all Navy and most Air Force activities under single commanders directly responsible to General Harkins and would eliminate the Military Assistance Advisory Group as an intervening command in the U.S. training and advisory mission in South Vietnam. After the advisory group was eliminated, the Military Assistance Program would come under MACV headquarters. General Harkins' plan also called for combining the special staff sections of the Military Assistance Command and the Military Assistance Advisory Group.

As the organization for the Military Assistance Program (MAP) ultimately developed within MACV headquarters, two staff directorates were established: the MAP Directorate and the Director of Army MAP Logistics. The former was a general policy, planning, and programming agency, and the latter assumed MAP logistic activities on a technical service basis.

In his comments on General Harkins' proposals to the Joint Chiefs, the new Commander in Chief, Pacific, Admiral U.S. Grant Sharp, Jr., who assumed command in February 1964, reiterated his predecessor's opposition to the merger of the two headquarters. He objected to the reorganization because it would tie the MACV commander to the details of the Military Assistance Program and the various advisory activities and prevent key members of the MACV staff from assuming positions in contingency operations. Admiral Sharp believed that establishing separate Naval and Air Force advisory groups would be tantamount to setting up two new uniservice Military Assistance Advisory Groups. He rejected General Harkins' basic concept—MACV as a specified Army command reporting to the Joint Chiefs, rather than as a subordinate unified command reporting to the Commander in Chief, Pacific—in the belief that the unified effort in Vietnam needed to be strengthened, not diluted. Admiral Sharp also noted that the proposed reorganization would greatly increase General Harkins' span of control—from five major subordinate elements to twelve or more—thereby multiplying command problems instead of reducing them.

Admiral Sharp proposed a more limited reorganization to the Joint Chiefs. He recommended that field advisers in Vietnam come under the control of the Military Assistance Command instead of the Military Assistance Advisory Group, which could then be reduced. The advisory group could continue to handle all MAP activities, including detailed planning and programming, and to

GENERAL WESTMORELAND

provide advisers to units—such as depots, schools, training centers, and administrative facilities—not directly involved in combat operations.

Early in April 1964 the Joint Chiefs approved the reorganization essentially as proposed by General Harkins. They did not, however, agree with his implied suggestion that MACV headquarters become an Army specified command, although they recognized that the headquarters would be heavily staffed with Army personnel. Finally, effective 15 May 1964, the Military Assistance Advisory Group was formally dissolved and the reorganized MACV headquarters was authorized. About a month later, on 20 June 1964, General William C. Westmoreland assumed command of the U.S. Military Assistance Command, Vietnam.

Another organizational issue concerned research, development, testing, and evaluation activities in South Vietnam. Admiral Felt had proposed a consolidation of these operations in 1963, and in February 1964 the Joint Chiefs established the Joint Research and Test Activity. This organization would control and supervise the several previously separate research and development agencies: the Department of Defense's Advanced Research Projects Agency Research and Development Field Unit; the U.S. Army Concept Team in Vietnam; the Air Force Test Unit, Vietnam; and the Joint Operations Evaluation Group, Vietnam. With the reorganization of MACV headquarters, the Joint Research and Test Activity acted as a joint agency under the operational control of the MACV commander. The Commander in Chief, Pacific, however, retained general responsibility for all research, development, testing, evaluation, and combat development activities throughout the Pacific Command.

Logistic Problems

The logistic system in Vietnam had failed to keep pace with rapidly expanding and increasingly complex support requirements. Army units under the operational control of the Military Assistance Command continued to receive combat service support from the

U.S. Army Support Command. The Navy's Headquarters, Support Activity, Saigon, established in 1962, continued to support MACV headquarters. Before the Military Assistance Advisory Group was dissolved, the support command assumed some of the logistic functions performed by the Army section, while the Navy's Support Activity in Saigon continued to provide countrywide support for Army advisory personnel.

Although U.S. strength in Vietnam grew from about 16,000 men (10,716 Army) to about 23,300 (16,000 Army) in 1964, logistic support operations were highly fragmented. Support for the U.S. Army came mainly from Okinawa and the continental United States; for the Marine Corps, from Japan and Okinawa; for the Navy, from the Philippines and Hawaii; and for the Air Force, largely from the Philippines. For example, there was no single logistic organization in Vietnam able to repair common-user items, such as vehicles, small arms, radios, generators, and office equipment. Transportation operations presented a particularly complex problem because personnel and equipment movements came under several transportation agencies. The search for ways to improve the logistic situation led to the next major change in the Army's command structure.

The major deficiency in logistic support operations in South Vietnam was the absence of an integrated logistic system. Although the Navy furnished logistic support to unified commands under the Pacific Command—a responsibility which Headquarters, Support Activity, Saigon, discharged for MACV headquarters—the Navy had neither the organizations nor the equipment to provide the growing level and diversity of support required. The Navy's support activity had been established in 1962 with duties limited to peacetime functions by the situation then existing in Vietnam, but it was not prepared to handle the kind and volume of support needed after 1963.

In addition to the support activity headquarters, the Navy was in charge of its own logistic system to support Navy personnel. Most Air Force logistic needs were filled by the 2d Air Division, and the Army was supplied by the U.S. Army Support Group, Vietnam. Other smaller military logistic support systems, as well as those of nonmilitary U.S. government agencies, were also operating in Vietnam. Finally, there was a commercial logistic agency operated by suppliers of petroleum, oil, and lubricants, who delivered their products to U.S. and Vietnamese forces under various civilian contracts. In all, fifteen separate logistic systems supported operations in Vietnam, supplying more than 150 locations where Americans were stationed. The logistic system reflected a lack of advance planning. The absence of a central logistic agency resulted in confusion that could be remedied only by organizational changes.

The 1st Logistical Command

Although various improvements in the logistic organization had been considered previously, it was early 1964 before the principal commanders and service chiefs involved agreed that an Army logistic command was needed in Vietnam. When the U.S. Army Support Group was created in 1962, one of its functions was to provide the nucleus for a type-B Army logistic command headquarters for contingency plans. When General Stilwell, the chief of the support group, also became the deputy Army component commander, his responsibilities increased to a point where his headquarters could not be expected to assume the additional duties of a logistic command. To solve this problem, a separate Army logistic command, deployed to Vietnam, was proposed.

Following a period of about three months, during which the strength, source of personnel, troop lists, and other related issues were worked out by the various headquarters concerned, Secretary of Defense McNamara approved the deployment of the 1st Logistical Command from the United States. An engineer group and the 1st Logistical Command were assigned to General Stilwell's command, which had been elevated from support group status to the U.S. Army Support Command, Vietnam, on 1 March 1964.

The 1st Logistical Command was originally established as a reduced type-A command. This meant it could command an integrated organization with a total strength of 9,000–15,000 men and could provide an organizational structure and a nucleus of trained logisticians and administrative personnel to support a major independent force of one reinforced division, approximately 30,000 men. Because of the U.S. buildup of forces in Vietnam, the 1st Logistical Command, on 10 July 1965, was authorized as a type-B command, one step up from type A, with a strength of 5,930 men. In accordance with its table of organization and equipment, this type of command could be augmented to a strength of 35,000–60,000 men in order to support an independent corps command, approximately 100,000 troops. The initial mission of the 1st Logistical Command was to provide support for all U.S. Army forces. As it grew, the command was gradually to take over the missions of Headquarters, Support Activity, Saigon, and assume responsibility on a phased basis for common-user supply services to all organizations of the U.S. and Free World Military Assistance Forces south of Chu Lai. The Navy was assigned the same task in the sector north of Chu Lai as far as the Demilitarized Zone.

By the end of 1965, in order to support the large number of U.S. combat elements introduced during the year, the strength of the 1st Logistical Command had increased to more than 22,000 men— over four times the projected estimate made a year earlier. Headquarters strength also grew from 159 men to 491. Toward the end of 1965 the 1st Logistical Command was mainly concerned with setting up subordinate logistic support areas at Qui Nhon, Nha Trang, and Vung Tau, and with developing the logistic depot and port complex at Cam Ranh Bay. The magnitude of the effort needed to establish this logistic base prevented the development of a common-item supply system and the shift of support activity functions to the Army.

Other Command Reorganizations

Beginning in March 1965, combat elements of the U.S. Marine Corps were deployed in the Da Nang area. When the III Marine Amphibious Force was established at Da Nang on 6 May, its commanding general, Major General William R. Collins, USMC, was designated the Naval component commander, a position previously held by the chief of the Naval Advisory Group, MACV. Later in the year, Rear Admiral Norvell G. Ward was appointed Chief, Naval Advisory Group, MACV. Since Admiral Ward, and not General Collins, directed the Navy's advisory effort as well as its coastal surveillance force, General Westmoreland, for all practical purposes, had two Naval component commanders for most of 1965.

On 25 June Major General Joseph H. Moore, USAF, who commanded the 2d Air Division and also served as the Air Force component commander, was made General Westmoreland's deputy commander for air operations at the grade of lieutenant general.

Although Air Force and Navy advisers operated under their component commanders—subject to general directives from the MACV commander—there was no central direction of the Army's advisory effort. Army advisory elements were widely dispersed. They served each of the four corps tactical zones of the Vietnamese Army, the ARVN Airborne Brigade, the Capital Military Region, and the Civilian Irregular Defense Group. In all, nine Army advisory groups reported directly to General Westmoreland.

On 10 July 1965, General Westmoreland's responsibility for military activities outside Vietnam was lessened when the positions of MACV commander and MACTHAI commander were separated. This action resulted from more than a year of discussions at the headquarters of the Pacific Command and at the Department of Defense. Military considerations—that Southeast Asia was a strategic entity and that fragmentation of command responsibilities would violate the basic principle of unity of command—tended to support continued adherence to a central command. Political considerations, on the other hand, such as Thailand's complaint that U.S. forces in Thailand were commanded from Saigon, suggested separation. The case for separation prevailed, and Major General Ernest F. Easterbrook, who was at the time both the deputy commander of MACTHAI and the chief of the Military Assistance Group in Thailand, was appointed Commander, Military Assistance Command, Thailand. General Easterbrook retained his position as chief of the assistance group in Thailand, and by the end of 1965 both headquarters were consolidated into one.

In early June 1965 a contingent of Australian and New Zealand forces arrived in Vietnam. Both were placed under General Westmoreland's operational control and attached to the 173d Airborne Brigade. Thus the precedent of placing Free World forces under the operational control of General Westmoreland was established and, later, followed by other nations. At no time, however, did General Westmoreland exercise operational control over the South Vietnamese armed forces.

The major buildup of U.S. Army combat forces and support activities that had begun early in 1965 required yet another reorganization. An Army headquarters was needed in Vietnam with capabilities far exceeding those of a logistical command. The issue of a separate Army component command was revived and eventually led to the decision to upgrade the U.S. Army Support Command and establish U.S. Army, Vietnam (USARV), in July 1965.

CHAPTER III

The Buildup of U.S. Forces:
July 1965–July 1966

In the Vietnam War, 1965 was a year of grave decisions. The North Vietnamese regarded the year as the beginning of the war's final phase, during which the Army of the Republic of Vietnam was to be destroyed by direct military action and the government and the people of South Vietnam were to lose their will to fight. The Communist hopes came close to being realized: the Saigon government had been weakened by a series of coups following the 1963 overthrow of President Diem; the Vietnamese armed forces had suffered a series of defeats that led to widespread demoralization; and government control, especially in the countryside, was eroding. The Viet Cong were expanding their power within the country, and beginning in 1965 the first North Vietnamese Army units in regimental strength were moving into the Central Highlands region. Enemy infiltration from the north was increasing and had reached a rate of more than one thousand men per month.

At this critical juncture, U.S. authorities came to the conclusion that the Vietnamese armed forces would no longer be able to contain the rising military threat to the security of their country without extensive additional military and economic assistance. This assistance, Ambassador Maxwell D. Taylor and General Westmoreland recommended, would have to include commitment of U.S. ground combat forces. President Lyndon B. Johnson decided to stand firmly behind the South Vietnamese people and defeat Communist aggression in Southeast Asia. Thus the year 1965, for the United States, was the year of military commitment.

The crucial events that occurred between July 1965 and July 1966 greatly affected the command and control arrangements in Vietnam. The rapid buildup of U.S. forces in Vietnam, the initiation of combat operations by U.S. forces, the expansion of logistical support operations, and the introduction of Free World Military Assistance Forces in a combat and combat support role all contributed to changes in a command structure that had originally been designed to accommodate only a U.S. military assistance mission.

AMBASSADOR TAYLOR

Essentially, there was change in the role and fun of the U.S. Ambassador to nam. General Taylor conti to have over-all responsi for all U.S. activities in Viet To assist the ambassador a provide a mechanism for level co-ordination and di sion, the Mission Council been formed in July 1964. Mission Council consisted o senior officials of the civil military elements of the Mission meeting together weekly basis. Under the c manship of the ambassa there was frank and com discussion of problems and posals covering the entire r of U.S. activities. General V moreland advised the council on military developments plans. New U.S. plans and programs were often proposed to se Vietnamese officials as they met periodically with the Mi Council. Thus the Mission Council was the policy-forming l of the United States in Saigon and gave co-ordinated guid and direction to all U.S. agencies in South Vietnam.

As mentioned earlier, doctrine for the U.S. armed forces scribed a separate Army component commander subordinat the unified commander; but as early as 1963 military planners determined that an Army component headquarters would be necessary and redundant. Instead, the joint force comman acting either as a U.S. or combined commander, should als his own Army component commander. An important consid tion supporting this arrangement was the desire to align the military structure in South Vietnam with that of the Vietnam armed forces. Since their Joint General Staff exercised operati control over the Vietnamese Army forces in the field, while h quarters of the Vietnamese Army had command less operati control, it was logical and practical for the MACV comma similarly to retain operational control of U.S. Army forces.

As a result, General Harkins, the MACV commander, had l designated the Army component commander in August 1963,

AMERICAN EMBASSY ANNEX BUILDING ON NGUYEN RUE IN DOWN-
TOWN SAIGON

the commander of the U.S. Army Support Group, Vietnam,
Brigadier General Joseph W. Stilwell, had been appointed the
deputy Army component commander. General Harkins thus exercised direct operational control over U.S. Army forces in Vietnam,
while General Stilwell retained command less operational control.
In March 1964, when the support group was redesignated U.S.
Army Support Command, Vietnam, this arrangement continued
unchanged.

U.S. Army, Vietnam

In late 1964 and early 1965, when a major buildup of U.S.
Army ground combat forces was imminent, planners from U.S.
Army, Pacific, and the Department of the Army began to restudy
current command arrangements. The ever-growing responsibilities
of the Army Support Command, especially its duties as the U.S.
Army component headquarters, precluded its reorganization into
a logistical command, as envisaged in contingency plans. The ob-

vious solution was to establish a separate logistical command. These developments strengthened the arguments of planners who wanted an Army headquarters to command U.S. Army ground forces.

In view of the possible deployment of major Army ground combat forces to Vietnam, the Army Chief of Staff, General Harold K. Johnson, recommended to the Joint Chiefs in March 1965 that a separate U.S. Army component command, under the operational control of the MACV commander, be established in Vietnam. Under his proposal, administrative and logistical functions concerning U.S. Army activities would be transferred from MACV headquarters to the new component command; the Army advisory effort would be similarly shifted, although the MACV commander would retain operational control. Under this arrangement, the Military Assistance Command would be relieved of administrative functions not directly related to combat or tactical operations.

The Commander in Chief, Pacific, Admiral Sharp, and the MACV commander, General Westmoreland, both opposed General Johnson's recommendation. On the other hand, MACV's Chief of Staff, Major General Richard G. Stilwell, held that an Army component command would prove to be a valuable co-ordinating link between the Military Assistance Command, the U.S. Army, Pacific, and the U.S. Army Support Command.

Through July 1965 there was a constant exchange of views between General Westmoreland and General John K. Waters, Commander in Chief, U.S. Army, Pacific, concerning the establishment of a separate Army component command under the Military Assistance Command. General Waters favored an Army component command with its own commander. General Westmoreland, however, made the following proposals: that the U.S. Army Support Command be redesignated U.S. Army, Vietnam (USARV); that he personally retain the responsibilities of the Army component commander and be made Commanding General, U.S. Army, Vietnam; that the incumbent commanding general of the U.S. Army Support Command be redesignated Deputy Commanding General, USARV; and that all Army units deployed to Vietnam be assigned to the USARV headquarters. General Westmoreland further recommended the establishment of several Army corps-level headquarters in Vietnam which, under his operational control, would conduct U.S. combat operations in their respective tactical zones. Westmoreland's proposals were approved by General Waters and the Department of the Army, and on 20 July 1965 a letter of instruction from U.S. Army, Pacific, headquarters spelled out the new command relationship.

The appointment of General Westmoreland as USARV's commanding general was a step away from the creation of a true Army component command. Although the MACV commander had been the Army component commander since August 1963, the senior Army headquarters in Vietnam had had its own commanding general. With the change of July 1965, both positions were occupied by the same individual, General Westmoreland. Thus he was put in the position of having to serve two masters: the Commander in Chief, Pacific, and the Commander in Chief, U.S. Army, Pacific. Similarly, U.S. Army organizations in Vietnam were responsible to the head of the Military Assistance Command for combat operations and to the commander in chief of U.S. Army, Pacific, for Army matters. The overlapping chains of command resulted in duplication and confusion within the MACV–USARV structure.

The command structure which evolved in Vietnam during 1965 bore striking resemblance to Army command arrangements that had existed in the Pacific and Europe during World War II and in the Korean War. During World War II General Douglas MacArthur had been both Commander in Chief, Southwest Pacific Area, and Commanding General, U.S. Army Forces in the Far East, the Army component. Operational control of U.S. Army combat forces had rested with General MacArthur as the commander of the Southwest Pacific Area, a position analogous to that of the MACV commander. Far East headquarters, however, had retained operational control over certain combat support and combat service support units not directly involved in the combat areas. The same situation had existed in Europe, where General Dwight D. Eisenhower, as Supreme Commander, Allied Expeditionary Force, had retained operational control over U.S. Army combat forces. General Eisenhower had also been his own Army component commander as commanding general of the European Theater of Operations.

During the Korean War General MacArthur had served as Commander in Chief, United Nations Command, and Commander in Chief, Far East. As such he had exercised direct operational control over U.S. Army combat forces in Korea. He had exercised command less operational control of all U.S. Army organizations in his role of Commanding General, U.S. Army Forces, Far East, a command generally analogous to U.S. Army Forces in the Far East and the European Theater of Operations in World War II and to U.S. Army, Vietnam. This arrangement had prevailed until after the prisoner of war riots at Koje-do in 1952, when General Mark Clark succeeded MacArthur as the Far East commander in chief

HEADQUARTERS OF THE U.S. ARMY, VIETNAM

and established a separate Army component—Army Forces, Far East. This arrangement lasted until the fighting stopped in 1953.

Field Forces, Vietnam

In March 1965 General Westmoreland had advised Admiral Sharp that if major U.S. ground combat forces were to be deployed to Vietnam, a combined corps-level field command would be needed. The MACV commander also indicated that he tentatively planned to designate his deputy as the commander of such a headquarters. Following discussions between the Military Assistance Command, the U.S. Army, Pacific, the Pacific Command, the Department of the Army, and the Joint Chiefs of Staff, Secretary of Defense McNamara in mid-May approved a combined field forces headquarters in Vietnam under the deputy MACV commander. However, further debate between the interested headquarters postponed its activation. Eventually, the Joint Chiefs approved deployment of a U.S. Army corps headquarters to Vietnam and directed the Army Chief of Staff, General Johnson, to develop the necessary plans. There were two main reasons for adopting the term "field force" rather than "corps" for the tactical corps-level headquarters about to be introduced into South Vietnam. First, as General Westmoreland pointed out, since the new headquarters was to operate in conformance with existing South Vietnamese corps zones, having two corps designations—one American and one South Vietnamese—in the same tactical zone would have been confusing. Second, the standard U.S. corps headquarters was a fixed organization. Field forces headquarters, on the other hand, would be more flexible and could be tailored to fit precisely the individual mission and could be adjusted to future changes, notably to further expansion of the U.S. effort.

Late in June, after further debate, the Joint Chiefs concluded that the field forces headquarters should be joint instead of Army. The Joint Chiefs believed that Westmoreland's plans envisaged control by this headquarters over U.S. and Free World ground combat organizations in both the I and II Corps Tactical Zones, thereby bringing the forces of the U.S. Marine Corps, U.S. Army, and Republic of Korea under one tactical corps-level command. The Joint Chiefs therefore directed Admiral Sharp, the Pacific commander in chief, to plan the organization of a joint field forces headquarters and to continue planning for the activation of a combined corps-level headquarters.

These instructions were confusing because two separate concepts for the field forces headquarters were entangled. In an effort to clarify the situation, General Westmoreland explained to Admiral Sharp that he intended the headquarters to be evolutionary. In the beginning, the field forces headquarters would be a small, provisional organization, to be known as Task Force Alpha, and would control only U.S. Army forces in the II Corps Tactical Zone. After the 1st Cavalry Division (Airmobile) reached Vietnam, Task Force Alpha would be expanded and designated Field Forces, Vietnam. In the event that Marine Corps forces in the I Corps Tactical Zone should come under the control of Field Forces, Vietnam, the headquarters could be augmented by Marine personnel. General Westmoreland contended that the headquarters should not include Navy or Air Force representation, since the support provided by these services would continue to be controlled by the Military Assistance Command. Westmoreland's proposal was adopted by the Joint Chiefs, and on 1 August 1965 Brigadier General Paul F. Smith temporarily assumed command of the newly activated Task Force Alpha until the arrival of the designated commander, Major General Stanley R. Larsen, on 4 August.

The Military Assistance Command gave the task force two missions: to exercise operational control over designated U.S. and Free World units and to provide combat support to South Vietnamese armed forces. In co-ordination with the Vietnamese commanding generals of the II and III Corps, Task Force Alpha would participate in the defense of U.S. and Vietnamese installations, conduct unilateral or combined offensive operations, and maintain close liaison with MACV's senior advisers at Vietnamese corps, division, and sector (province) levels. These advisers would be the task force's principal points of contact with Vietnamese troops. General Westmoreland emphasized that the relationship between the commanding general of the task force and the Vietnamese Army corps commanders would be one of co-ordination and co-operation.

Task Force Alpha was redesignated Field Forces, Vietnam, on 25 September 1965, as plans were being made for a second Army corps-level headquarters in Vietnam. This plan was approved by Secretary of Defense McNamara in December 1965, and Field Forces, Vietnam, was redesignated I Field Force, Vietnam. The new corps-level headquarters was designated II Field Force, Vietnam, and assigned responsibility for the III Corps zone.

The U.S. Marine Corps

Viet Cong attacks against U.S. installations at Pleiku and Qui Nhon early in 1965 had prompted President Johnson to order the evacuation of all dependents of U.S. government officials in Vietnam. Meanwhile, General Westmoreland and the Joint Chiefs discussed sending a Marine expeditionary brigade and additional Army forces to Da Nang and other critical locations in Vietnam. The Joint Chiefs recommended to Secretary McNamara that the Marine brigade be committed and that additional Air Force tactical squadrons be moved to the western Pacific and to Vietnam. General Westmoreland agreed, but he advised Admiral Sharp and the Joint Chiefs that more security forces might be needed, especially in Da Nang, in the Saigon–Bien Hoa–Vung Tau area, and in the Nha Trang–Cam Ranh Bay complex. There had been some discussion between General Westmoreland, Admiral Sharp, and the Joint Chiefs over the possibility of sending the Army's 173d Airborne Brigade instead of the Marine's brigade. The 9th Marine Expeditionary Brigade was selected, however, and the leading elements went ashore on 8 March. The original mission of the brigade was entirely security-oriented, and the force was directed not to engage in day-to-day offensive operations against the Viet Cong.

Early in March 1965, General Westmoreland proposed a significant change in basic U.S. policy in Vietnam. In response to an inquiry from the Joint Chiefs of Staff, the MACV commander noted that the only way to forestall a Viet Cong take-over of the country—except in the major population centers that were under the control of the government of Vietnam—was to commit additional U.S. and Free World forces. These forces would have to be prepared to perform whatever military operations were needed. General Westmoreland's proposal was supported by Admiral Sharp and the Joint Chiefs, and in the next several weeks an accelerated planning effort was undertaken involving all four service departments, as well as the Joint Chiefs, Admiral Sharp, and General Westmoreland. The resulting strategy, to be carried out by the Pacific Command, called for U.S. forces to secure coastal enclaves from which they could engage in operations against the enemy in co-ordination with the Vietnamese armed forces, and where they could build major logistical bases to support future combined offensive operations. Strategy also dictated that the following force groupings be sent to Vietnam: a U.S. Marine Corps division (supported by an air wing), tentatively designated III Marine Expeditionary Force, to be deployed in the I Corps Tactical Zone; and U.S. Army and Free World forces, to be deployed in the II and III Corps areas. Such an arrangement would provide for a comparatively simple operational chain of command extending directly from the Military Assistance Command to the III Marine Expeditionary Force in the I Corps zone, and to the two Army field forces headquarters in the Vietnamese II and III Corps zones.

Late in 1965 these plans were modified to include two U.S. Marine Corps divisions and their organic air wings in the I Corps Tactical Zone under the commanding general of the III Marine Amphibious Force, as well as additional U.S. Army forces for the II and III Corps zones. The basic concept for operational control of these forces remained unchanged. In South Vietnam the Marine Corps would be responsible for a geographic area of operations equivalent to the I Corps Tactical Zone under the operational control of General Westmoreland, while the U.S. Army would have similar assignments in II and III Corps zones. In the Mekong Delta the existing advisory structure remained in force. With the exception of some modifications for the delta area—the Vietnamese IV Corps Tactical Zone—these arrangements prevailed until the 1968 *Tet* offensive, which prompted significant U.S. reinforcement of the I Corps Tactical Zone. (*Chart 5*)

CHART 5—MILITARY ASSISTANCE COMMAND, VIETNAM, 1965

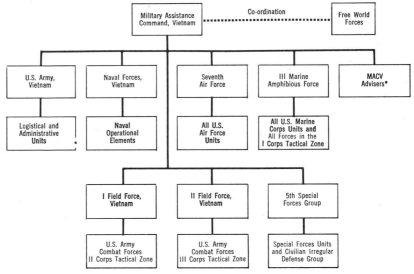

* Except those MACV advisers who double as commanders of U.S. troop units

Source: Report on the War in Vietnam (as of 30 June 1968) by Admiral U.S. Grant Sharp, USN, and General William C. Westmoreland, USA (Washington: 1969), Section II, Chapter III, p. 102.

Organization of Advisory Effort

Command and control of U.S. military advisers was exercised in two separate and distinct ways. For Navy and Air Force advisers, the chain of command ended with the respective service component commanders at the MACV level. In the case of the Navy, the commander of the Naval Advisory Group reported directly to the Naval component commander, who was the Commander, U.S. Naval Forces, Vietnam; a single individual filled both positions. In the case of the Air Force, the chief of the Air Force Advisory Group at MACV headquarters was also the commanding general of the 2d Air Division as well as the Air Force component commander in Vietnam. In other words, the advisory efforts of the Navy and the Air Force were under the operational control of their respective service component commanders, who received direction and guidance from General Westmoreland.

Army advisers, on the other hand, were under the operational control of the MACV commander. During 1965 a total of nine U.S.

Army advisory groups reported directly to General Westmoreland, the MACV commander, rather than to the headquarters of the Army component commander, U.S. Army, Vietnam. These groups included separate advisory elements for the ARVN Airborne Brigade; the Regional and Popular Forces; the Railway Security Advisory Detachment; the Capital Military Region; the Civilian Irregular Defense Group, advisory effort of the 5th Special Forces Group; and each of the four Vietnamese Army corps.

With the introduction of U.S. ground combat forces and the establishment of U.S. Army corps-level headquarters in South Vietnam, modifications in the control of U.S. Army advisory efforts became essential. Following the arrival of the III Marine Amphibious Force in the I Corps Tactical Zone, the advisory group to the I Corps was placed under the operational control of the commanding general of the Marine amphibious force, who was designated the senior adviser to the I Vietnamese Corps commander. The previous senior adviser, an Army colonel, became the deputy senior adviser. In practice this new arrangement caused few changes, since the deputy senior adviser continued to operate much as he had in the past, employing both U.S. Army and Marine Corps officers and enlisted men as advisers. At the headquarters of the III Marine Amphibious Force, the advisory effort thus could not be considered a fully integrated operation within the command structure.

To the south, in the II and III Corps zones of the Vietnamese Army, similar arrangements developed. In the II Corps, after Task Force Alpha had been formed and given operational control of all U.S. forces, Army advisory personnel remained under MACV's operational control. When the task force was replaced by Field Forces, Vietnam, the Vietnamese II Corps' commanding general expressed annoyance that the senior U.S. Army officer in his area, who was the commanding general of the Field Forces, was not also his senior adviser. Accordingly, in October 1965, General Larsen, the Field Forces' commander, was appointed the senior adviser to the II Corps' commanding general; and—as was the case with the III Marine Amphibious Force—the former senior adviser, also an Army colonel, became the deputy senior adviser. The same arrangements were made in the III Corps zone, with the commanding general of the 1st Infantry Division acting as the senior adviser.

Since no major U.S. forces were introduced into the IV Corps area, the advisory group there continued under the operational control of the MACV commander, General Westmoreland.

Control of U.S. Operating Forces

Throughout 1965, control of all U.S. Air Force elements in Vietnam was exercised by the service's component commander. The commanding general of the 2d Air Division, Lieutenant General Joseph H. Moore, was both the component commander and the chief of the U.S. Air Force Advisory Group at MACV headquarters. In May 1965 General Moore was designated General Westmoreland's deputy commander for air operations, a position not to be confused with the Deputy Commander, Military Assistance Command, who had always been an Army general officer.

Air operations against North Vietnam were controlled by the Pacific commander in chief through the commander of the Pacific Air Forces and, in the case of U.S. Navy air forces, through the commander of the Pacific Fleet. Thus General Moore exercised operational control over Air Force units in Southeast Asia as directed by the Pacific Air Forces commander; for air operations over South Vietnam, he was guided by directives from General Westmoreland.

At the beginning of 1965, the component commander for U.S. naval forces in Vietnam was also the chief of MACV's Naval Advisory Group. With the arrival of Marine Corps ground combat forces in March, the commanding general of the 9th Marine Expeditionary Brigade became the naval component commander; the commanding general of the III Marine Amphibious Force assumed this role when his headquarters came ashore in May. This arrangement was modified after the Coastal Surveillance Force (TF 115) was created in July. Both the advisory group and the Coastal Surveillance Force then came under the Chief, Naval Advisory Group, whose title became Commander, U.S. Naval Forces, Vietnam–Chief, Naval Advisory Group. Thus, General Westmoreland actually had two naval component commanders: one for conventional Navy forces and one for Marine Corps elements.

Except for the Marine Corps command, the arrival of additional U.S. Navy and Air Force troops caused no significant change in the existing command and control structure in Vietnam. With each of these two services organized as a separate component under the Military Assistance Command, the respective commanders reported directly to General Westmoreland for operational matters and through their service chains of command for all other matters.

Throughout 1965, as in 1964, General Westmoreland had subordinate Air Force and Navy component commanders in South Vietnam but acted as his own Army component commander. The Air Force and Navy component commanders had operational control over their component forces, as General Westmoreland had over Army forces. This arrangement was compatible with the command and control system of the Vietnamese Army, in which operational control of army forces rested with the South Vietnamese Joint General Staff.

Co-ordination with Vietnamese and Free World Forces

Before the Free World Military Assistance Forces came to Vietnam, there had been no need for a combined or multinational command. As U.S. and other Free World forces began arriving in South Vietnam in April 1965, however, General Westmoreland recommended establishing a small, combined U.S.–South Vietnamese headquarters, commanded by a U.S. general officer with a Vietnamese deputy or chief of staff. For political reasons, General Westmoreland believed that such a headquarters would have to be introduced gradually and quietly. He also recommended forming an international military security task force as a low-level combined staff in the Da Nang area.

The idea of a combined command appeared to be favored by senior Vietnamese commanders when it was first suggested in April 1965. This attitude, however, was soon replaced by extreme sensitivity to the subject. When this change became apparent, the United States no longer pursued the matter of a combined command, and General Westmoreland withdrew his earlier recommendations, including those concerning the security task force. Instead, U.S. field commanders were instructed to work with Vietnamese commanders on the basis of co-operation and co-ordination, rather than through a traditional combined command arrangement. To ensure close liaison with the Military Assistance Command, General Westmoreland appointed Brigadier General James L. Collins, Jr., as his special representative to the Joint General Staff of the Vietnamese armed forces.

Only in the area of intelligence was there a combined or integrated effort between U.S. and Vietnamese forces. To take the best advantage of the resources and information of both, the Combined Intelligence Center, Vietnam, was formed. The center had four major functions: interrogation of prisoners, exploitation of captured enemy material, exploitation of captured documents, and the preparation of intelligence reports for both U.S. and Vietnamese commands. As U.S. troop strength rose and military operations became more extensive, the number of documents, prisoners, and North Vietnamese Army and Viet Cong deserters increased. Consequently, the volume of intelligence data also grew. Pooling the resources at the Combined Intelligence Center, therefore, permitted a more efficient use of the limited number of specialists and a faster dissemination of information.

The introduction of Free World Military Assistance Forces into South Vietnam raised the question of their command and control. Two separate arrangements were developed. For troops provided by countries other than the Republic of Korea, operational control rested with the U.S. military commander in whose area these troops were used. In the case of the South Korean forces, a compromise was worked out between U.S., Korean, and Vietnamese officials by which these forces would remain under their own control, within the limits established by a council to be known as the Free World Military Assistance Council. The council consisted of the MACV commander, the commander of the Republic of Korea Forces, Vietnam, and the chief of the Vietnamese Joint General Staff, who served as chairman.

Logistic Support

As early as 1962 the MACV commander had seen the need for a central logistical organization in South Vietnam and had recommended that a U.S. Army logistical command be sent to Vietnam. It was late April 1965, however, before the Secretary of Defense formally approved the establishment of an Army logistical command for Vietnam. On 10 July 1965, the 1st Logistical Command was authorized as a full-strength, type-B command. By the end of the year the command had grown from 5,930 men to more than 22,000. It supported all U.S. and Free World forces south of Chu Lai. The sector to the north was a Navy responsibility.

Communications-Electronics

During the initial buildup phase, communications systems in Vietnam were inadequate to perform the tasks facing the Military Assistance Command. Early in 1965, General Westmoreland, in conjunction with the director of the Defense Communications Agency, Lieutenant General Alfred D. Starbird, requested a consolidation of communications-electronics functions at the MACV level. This proposal was approved by the Joint Chiefs of Staff in April 1965; an office of the Defense Communications Agency would be established in Vietnam under the MACV Communications-Electronics Directorate (J–6).

To supplement this joint management, all Army communications-electronics resources in Vietnam were combined in a single command, the 1st Signal Brigade. Established in April 1966, it supported the combat signal battalions of the divisions and field forces in each corps area. Additionally, the 1st Signal Brigade operated the many elements of the Defense Communications System in Vietnam. To improve co-ordination and management of communications-electronics assets, the commander of the 1st Signal Brigade also served as the U.S. Army, Vietnam, staff adviser on all matters pertaining to Army communications-electronics.

Analysis

Command and control in Vietnam has been a matter of controversy since U.S. ground forces were introduced in 1965. Critics have contended that the Vietnam War required clearer lines of command authority and greater subordination of individual service efforts to the control of a single commander. From among their recommended improvements, three significant alternative command structures emerged: a single combined command exercising operational control of all Free World forces, including the South Vietnamese; a separate unified command, directly subordinate to the Joint Chiefs of Staff, controlling all U.S. forces in Vietnam; and a separate U.S. Army component command, under the Military Assistance Command, exercising operational control of all U.S. ground forces in the Vietnam conflict.

A combined command offered significant advantages in major combat operations, was supported by precedents set in World War II and Korea, and applied the principle of unity of command. However, the nature of the Vietnam conflict and the international political situation when the United States initiated combat operations were such that the benefits of a "supreme allied command" would have been canceled out by charges of U.S. colonialism and by difficulties inherent in a future reduction of U.S. forces. A major obstacle to a combined command arrangement was the reluctance of South Vietnam and South Korea to relinquish sovereignty over their armed forces. General Westmoreland recognized these problems. His decision to forgo the advantages of a combined command has been proven sound by subsequent events.

The proponents of a separate unified command contended that eliminating the Commander in Chief, Pacific, from the chain of command would have simplified the direction of the war from Washington and eased the burdens of the commander in Vietnam. This argument was refuted by General Westmoreland, who maintained that the duties performed by the Commander in Chief, Pacific, and the service component commanders allowed him to focus his primary attention on operations in Vietnam, while his

MACV HEADQUARTERS COMPLEX NEAR TAN SON NHUT, *1969.*

lines of communication to the rear were secured and managed by the Pacific Command. A more valid objection to this proposition, however, was the fact that the war in Vietnam could not be considered as an isolated conflict. While the ground fighting was largely confined to South Vietnam, the threat of hostilities elsewhere in Southeast Asia required a contingency planning and response capability available only to the Commander in Chief, Pacific. Therefore, only a division of responsibility between the Commander, U.S. Military Assistance Command, and the Commander in Chief, Pacific, ensured effective management of the war in South Vietnam and preparedness for other contingencies in Southeast Asia.

Early creation of a U.S. Army component under the Military Assistance Command, with operational control of combat forces and responsibility for fighting the ground war, might have been preferable to existing command arrangements. During 1964 and 1965, however, the advantages of such an arrangement were not evident. U.S. ground combat forces were originally introduced to provide security for an existing organization. Only after the situation deteriorated were these forces compelled to conduct limited offensive operations. General Westmoreland had the choice either to retain the established and satisfactory method of operation, or to create an additional command headquarters between his MACV headquarters and the combat forces. He decided to retain the existing arrangement and to exercise operational control personally, not only because this method worked but also because his command was designed to match the organization of the Vietnamese armed forces. The absence of a combined command in Vietnam made co-operation and co-ordination among Free World forces a primary concern. From the U.S. point of view, co-operation and co-ordination could be maintained effectively only if the Military Assistance Command, like its Vietnamese counterpart the Joint General Staff, had full operational control of ground forces, and liaison between the two commanders was as close as possible.

CHAPTER IV

The Continuing Buildup: July 1966–July 1969

By mid-1966 U.S. forces in South Vietnam numbered about 276,000 men, 166,000 of them Army. In March the headquarters of II Field Force, Vietnam, had been activated under the command of Major General Jonathan O. Seaman at the same time that Major General Stanley R. Larsen's headquarters was redesignated I Field Force, Vietnam. In April 1966 the 2d Air Division was elevated to Seventh Air Force, and U.S. Naval Forces, Vietnam, was established. With these changes, the command structure had matured to its full growth and henceforth was to undergo adaptation rather than major structural change until well after President Nixon announced the withdrawal of U.S. forces in June 1969. (*Chart 6*)

Pacification

A major organizational development during this period was the consolidation of the efforts of all U.S. agencies involved in Vietnamese pacification programs. Centralization of many diverse programs did not come easily, quickly, or even completely, but observers realized that a united effort was necessary in order to achieve better co-ordination among U.S. military and civilian agencies concerned with pacification. Especially important to success in this effort was the development of an organization that could effectively direct all programs after they were brought under the over-all control of the Military Assistance Command in the spring of 1967.

Shortly before General Westmoreland became the MACV commander he visited Kuala Lumpur, Malaya, in the company of Sir Robert G. K. Thompson, head of the British Advisory Mission to Vietnam, Alfred M. Hurt, Director of the United States Overseas Mission (later designated the U.S. Agency for International Development), and Barry Zorthian, head of the Joint U.S. Public Affairs Office in Vietnam. The group spent several days studying the organization and techniques used by British and Malayan leaders during the Communist insurgency in the 1950s. On-the-

AMBASSADOR LODGE

spot observations confirmed the assumption that unity of command in the U.S. pacification effort in Vietnam was needed at the province level. Essentially, a single American "team captain" was required, who would act as the principal adviser to the province chief and be in charge of both civil and military matters.

Although the Vietnamese and the Americans were aware that successful pacification required both the restoration of security and the development of the nation, progress toward these objectives had been limited during 1964 and 1965. In 1965 the Vietnamese changed the term "pacification" to "rural reconstruction" and later to "rural construction." By the end of the year they had developed the concept of rural construction cadres. These cadres were to consist of highly motivated, specially trained teams that would move into hamlets, defend them, and initiate development programs. A decision was made to train eighty of these teams in 1966.

While the Vietnamese were attempting to make their pacification efforts more effective, the Americans were striving to improve U.S. support of these activities. The total U.S. effort involved several independent civil agencies as well as the military, but U.S. actions were not well co-ordinated. In January 1966 a meeting was held near Washington, D.C., to study ways of improving U.S. support for rural construction activities. Senior representatives from all agencies of the U.S. Mission in Saigon, from the Washington Vietnam Coordinating Committee, and from other U.S. government agencies attended. The meeting revealed that all agencies recognized the need for improved co-ordination of U.S. pacification efforts and that they favored the development of pacification and the training of cadres. Shortly thereafter, Ambassador Henry Cabot Lodge appointed Deputy Ambassador William J. Porter as co-ordinator of U.S. activities in support of rural construction and charged him to reconcile roles and duties within the U.S. Mission.

In February 1966 the Vietnamese Ministry of Rural Construction was redesignated the Ministry of Construction to dispel the

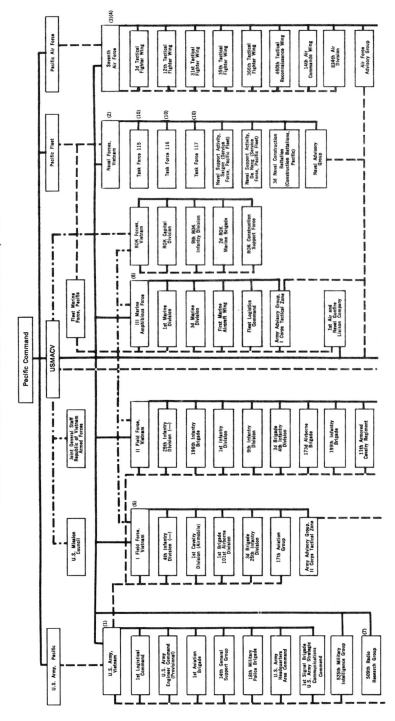

CHART 6—PACIFIC COMMAND RELATIONSHIPS, 1967

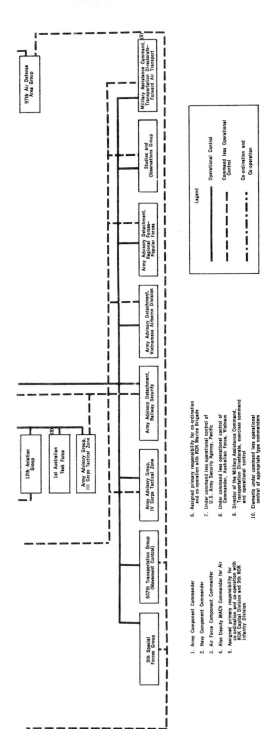

97th Air Defense Area Group

Military Assistance Command, Transportation Directorate-Forward Air Transport (9)

Studies and Observations Group

Army Advisory Detachment, Regional Forces-Popular Forces

Army Advisory Detachment, Vietnamese Airborne Division

Army Advisory Detachment, Railway Security

12th Aviation Group

1st Australian Task Force (8)

Army Advisory Group, III Corps Tactical Zone

Army Advisory Group, IV Corps Tactical Zone

507th Transportation Group (Movement Control)

5th Special Forces Group

Legend

——————— Operational Control

– – – – – Command less Operational Control

–··–··– Co-ordination and Co-operation

1. Army Component Commander
2. Navy Component Commander
3. Air Force Component Commander
4. Also Deputy MACV Commander for Air
5. Assigned primary responsibility for co-ordination and co-operation with ROK Capital Division and 9th ROK Infantry Division
6. Assigned primary responsibility for co-ordination and co-operation with ROK Marine Brigade
7. Under command less operational control of U.S. Army Security Agency, Pacific
8. Under command less operational control of Commander, Australian Force, Vietnam
9. Director of the Military Assistance Command, Transportation Directorate, exercises command and operational control
10. Elements under command less operational control of appropriate type commanders

Source: USMACV Command History, 1967, Vol. I, p. 123.

mistaken idea that urban areas were excluded from this agency's concern. Because the Vietnamese translation did not make this distinction clear, Premier Nguyen Cao Ky coined the term "revolutionary development" (RD) to describe the mission of the ministry. In more definitive terms, the U.S. and Vietnamese governments agreed on the following statement:

RD is the integrated military and civil process to restore, consolidate and expand government control so that nation building can progress throughout the Republic of Vietnam. It consists of those coordinated military and civil actions to liberate the people from Viet Cong control; restore public security; initiate political, economic and social development; extend effective Government of Vietnam authority; and win the willing support of people toward these ends.

In order to consolidate the U.S. civilian pacification effort further, Ambassador Lodge established the Office of Civil Operations in November 1966. L. Wade Lathram was named the first director; he was responsible to Deputy Ambassador Porter for U.S. civilian activities in support of revolutionary development and U.S. civil operations in the pacification program. At the same time, General Westmoreland elevated the MACV Revolutionary Development Support Division (created in late 1964 to co-ordinate military support of pacification) to directorate level, increased the staff, and named a general officer as director. To strengthen civil-military co-ordination, Major General Paul F. Smith was put in charge of revolutionary development in the office of Deputy Ambassador Porter. He was directly responsible for maintaining liaison with the Military Assistance Command in matters pertaining to U.S. and Vietnamese military support of the program. Directors for four regions—the Vietnamese corps areas—were appointed by Ambassador Lodge in December 1966. General Westmoreland directed the commanding generals of the III Marine Amphibious Force and of the I and II Field Forces and the senior adviser to the IV Corps to give all necessary assistance to the regional directors.

Despite these measures, effective integration of civil and military activities in support of the revolutionary development program remained an elusive goal. A major problem was the lack of personnel in the civilian agencies—the Joint U.S. Public Affairs Office, the U.S. Agency for International Development, and the Office of the Special Assistant—to work at the province (sector) and district (subsector) levels. In fact, the only permanent U.S. advisers at the district level were those of the Military Assistance Command.

It was at the district and province levels that pacification had to begin and be made to work. Since military advisers were predominant at those levels and pacification depended on military security, integration of the civilian and military efforts was essential. Realizing this urgent need, President Johnson, in conferences with President Thieu and other South Vietnamese leaders at Guam in March 1967, decided to integrate the civilian and military U.S. support efforts under General Westmoreland. This decision heralded a major change in U.S. command arrangements that would have a lasting effect on the combined pacification effort.

On the part of the United States, the first organizational and personnel changes came with the arrival in Saigon of Ambassador Ellsworth Bunker,

AMBASSADOR BUNKER

who replaced Ambassador Lodge in April 1967. Deputy Ambassador Porter was succeeded in office by Eugene M. Locke. In addition, Presidential Assistant Robert W. Komer, who had been overseeing revolutionary development support activities at the Washington level since March 1966, was assigned to General Westmoreland's headquarters. In May 1967, Ambassador Bunker announced that the U.S. Mission's responsibility for the revolutionary development program was being integrated under the Military Assistance Command in a single-manager arrangement, and that General Westmoreland would assume the responsibility under the over-all authority of the ambassador. There were two basic reasons for assigning the task to General Westmoreland. First, security, a prerequisite to pacification, was a primary responsibility of the Vietnamese armed forces, which were advised by the Military Assistance Command—Westmoreland's headquarters. Second, the greater part of U.S. advisory and logistic resources were under General Westmoreland's control.

Presidential Assistant Komer was appointed Westmoreland's deputy for Civil Operations and Rural Development Support (CORDS) with the rank of ambassador, and the four regional directors of the Office of Civil Operations were assigned as deputies to the four senior advisers to the Vietnamese corps. The Embassy's Office of Civil Operations and MACV's Revolutionary Development Support Directorate (RDSD) merged to form, within the

AMERICAN EMBASSY ON THONG NGAI STREET IN DOWNTOWN SAIGON

Military Assistance Command, the office of Assistant Chief of Staff for CORDS. Mr. Lathram, who had been the director of the Civil Operations office, was given this new position, and Brigadier General William A. Knowlton, who had been the RDSD director, became his deputy. Of the resulting arrangement, Ambassador Bunker said: "Such a unified civil-military US advisory effort in the vital field of RD is unprecedented. . . . RD is in my view neither civil nor military but a unique merging of both to meet a unique wartime need." Thus the single-manager concept had become a reality. It was based on the realization that the pacification effort and the war fought in the field were inseparable elements of the Vietnam conflict.

On the part of the Vietnamese, organizational changes were more slowly realized than in the U.S. camp. At the national level the government of South Vietnam, in November 1967, established the Central Revolutionary Development Council, headed by the Prime Minister. Members of the Central Council were the heads of the key ministries responsible for the many aspects of the pacification programs, notably the Ministers of Defense, Interior, Public

Works, Land Reform and Agriculture, Health, Refugees, and *Chieu Hoi* and the commander in chief of the army and all corps commanders. The Minister of Revolutionary Development served as Secretary General and his ministry was the Central Council's executive agency. Throughout South Vietnam, Regional Revolutionary Development Councils were formed at the corps, special zone, provincial and municipal, and district levels. Thus, by the end of 1967, a revolutionary development network was established that would put the country's human and material resources to work on the pacification effort.

The revolutionary development network, however, was not wholly complementary to the U.S. single-manager concept for pacification. The reason was the special position of the South Vietnamese province chief in the chain of command. Traditionally, the province chief was charged with security as well as general administration of all government services within his province. Appointed by the president, he was responsible to the president for his province and had direct access to the president at all times. As far as national policy and government programs were concerned, the province chief was responsible to the Prime Minister, and regarding general administration, to the Minister of the Interior. In addition, the province chief was subject to pressures from the corps commander and the division commander in his area. In a very real sense, the province chief was constantly faced with conflicts of authority that were damaging to the national administrative machinery. To a lesser degree, this situation also applied to the district chiefs.

The integration of revolutionary development support under the Military Assistance Command and the staff realignments that resulted had a profound influence on the U.S. advisory effort. First, a single U.S. team chief was appointed for each province. In mid-1967, when the program got under way, twenty-five of these province senior advisers were military and nineteen were civilian. Second, the MACV subsector (district) advisory team became the nucleus of the CORDS staff at the district level. The district staff now included both military and civilian personnel, and its chief was responsible for the management of support activities pertaining to revolutionary development. The head of the team was redesignated the district senior adviser. Finally, staff elements at the field force and Marine Amphibious Force levels, which had previously been engaged in support activities, were each integrated into separate CORDS staff offices. Each CORDS office dealt directly with the province senior advisers within the corps tactical zones regarding military operations related to the revolutionary development program. Thus, at the field force level the deputy senior

Chart 7—CORDS Field Organization

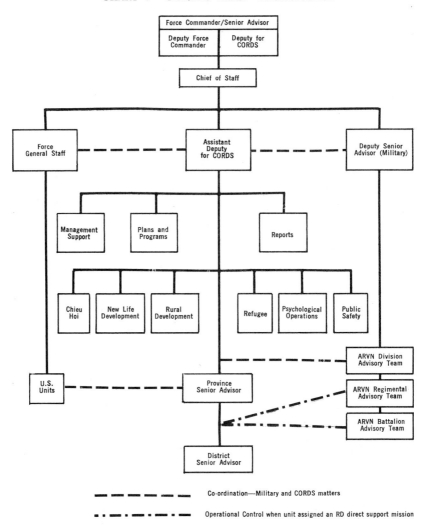

Force Commander/Senior Advisor

Deputy Force Commander | Deputy for CORDS

Chief of Staff

Force General Staff — Assistant Deputy for CORDS — Deputy Senior Advisor (Military)

Management Support | Plans and Programs | Reports

Chieu Hoi | New Life Development | Rural Development | Refugee | Psychological Operations | Public Safety

ARVN Division Advisory Team

U.S. Units — Province Senior Advisor — ARVN Regimental Advisory Team

ARVN Battalion Advisory Team

District Senior Advisor

————— Co-ordination—Military and CORDS matters

—·—·—·— Operational Control when unit assigned an RD direct support mission

Source: USMACV Command History, 1967, Vol. II, p. 589.

adviser (a military officer, not to be confused with the Civil Operations regional director, who had been designated deputy for CORDS) ceased to exercise command supervision over the province (sector) advisory teams within the corps zone. The deputy senior adviser did, however, continue to be responsible for the advisory activities of military units. Thus, two separate chains of command developed: one for military and civil advisory efforts pertaining to pacification, and one for military advisory efforts pertaining to Vietnamese units. These field relationships remained essentially unchanged from 1967 onward. (*Chart 7*)

Response to the Communist Threat in the North

Following the introduction of major U.S. forces in South Vietnam in 1965, there was a gradual buildup of enemy forces in the northern part of the I Corps Tactical Zone. To counter this threat, the I Corps area was reinforced as much as possible from U.S., Vietnamese, and Free World forces already in South Vietnam. In August 1966 the Republic of Korea Marine Brigade was moved from the II Corps area to the southern part of the I Corps. This action permitted greater concentration of U.S. 1st Marine Division forces in the Da Nang area, allowing in turn the concentration of the 3d Marine Division in the two northernmost provinces. During early 1967, further concentration of forces in the northern part of the I Corps area was carried out by moving more units from the central and southern parts closer to the Demilitarized Zone.

By April 1967, increased enemy activity prompted General Westmoreland to form Task Force OREGON and send it to the southern part of the I Corps zone, thereby freeing additional U.S. Marine units to move farther north. Task Force OREGON was comprised of a provisional headquarters, division support troops from various U.S. Army units, and three brigades taken from areas where they could be spared with the least risk. These brigades were the 196th Light Infantry Brigade from the III Corps area, and the 1st Brigade of the 101st Airborne Division and the 3d Brigade of the 25th Infantry Division (subsequently redesignated the 3d Brigade of the 4th Infantry Division) from the II Corps zone. Later in the year, the 3d Brigade of the 25th Division and the 1st Brigade of the 101st Division were replaced by the newly arrived 198th and 11th Light Infantry Brigades. In September 1967 Task Force OREGON became the 23d Infantry Division (Americal).

The original plan for reinforcing the I Corps zone called for U.S. Army forces to conduct operations south of Da Nang, allowing the U.S. Marines to concentrate farther north. This division of responsibility according to sectors was designed to avoid operational and logistic confusion, but the concept had to be abandoned when the enemy buildup along the Demilitarized Zone and in Laos increased to the point where further U.S. deployments to the area were needed. General Westmoreland moved U.S. Army forces to the middle of the northern I Corps area to support the U.S. Marines, with the result that units of the two services intermixed and the command and control structure became overburdened. To relieve the situation, the headquarters of the 1st Cavalry Division was moved north early in 1968. More U.S. Army units followed. The 2d Brigade, 101st Airborne Division, moved to the vicinity of Hue in January, and in February both the 27th Marine Regimental Landing Team and the 3d Brigade, 82d Airborne Division, were airlifted from the United States to the I Corps Tactical Zone.

The controlling and planning capability of the III Marine Amphibious Force headquarters became severely taxed by the presence of these additional Army and Marine forces. General Westmoreland responded to the command and control problem by establishing MACV Forward headquarters in the Hue–Phu Bai area on 9 February 1968. From the new headquarters, General Creighton W. Abrams, the deputy MACV commander, exercised control for General Westmoreland over all joint combat and logistical forces—Army, Navy, Air Force, and Marine—deployed in the northern I Corps area. These forces were being assembled to meet a major enemy offensive, which was expected in Quang Tri Province.

One month later on 10 March 1968, MACV Forward, having served its purpose, was converted to a corps headquarters and designated Provisional Corps, Vietnam, under the command of Lieutenant General William B. Rosson. General Rosson exercised operational control over the 3d Marine Division (Reinforced), the 1st Cavalry Division, the 101st Airborne Division (−) (Reinforced), and assigned corps troops. The new corps also co-operated closely with the Vietnamese 1st Division in the area.

The I Corps zone was divided into two parts by a boundary through Thua Thien Province that ran roughly north of Da Nang. The Provisional Corps, Vietnam, which was designated XXIV Corps on 12 August 1968, had operational control over ground tactical units north of the boundary, while the III Marine Amphibious Force exercised operational control of the corps in the north and of all tactical units south of the boundary. Thus freed from the task of directing the battle in the north on a day-to-day basis, the commanding general of the Marine amphibious force, Lieutenant General Robert E. Cushman, Jr., USMC, was able to concentrate

GENERAL ROSSON. (*Photograph taken after his promotion to four-star general.*)

GENERAL MOMYER

on the entire I Corps area, especially on CORDS functions and logistic support responsibilities.

As operations in the north expanded, General Westmoreland decided that an important adjustment in the tactical aircraft control system in the I Corps area was needed. Before 1968 there had been two managers for air assets in the I Corps zone: the deputy MACV commander for air operations, who was also the commander of the Seventh Air Force, had operational control of the Seventh Air Force's men and equipment and of any Navy air support from Task Force 77; and the commanding general of the III Marine Amphibious Force had operational control of the resources of the 1st Marine Aircraft Wing. This air unit supported the U.S. Marines in the I Corps area, while the Seventh Air Force supported U.S. Army units, the Korean marine brigade, and the Vietnamese forces. General Westmoreland considered it "of paramount importance to achieve a single manager for control of tactical air resources"; therefore, on 8 March 1968 he appointed his deputy for air operations, General William W. Momyer, as manager of all air assets. The system for tactical air support was adjusted to conform with the new ground organizational structure and became effective on 1 April 1968. (*Chart 8*)

The terrain and enemy activity in the I Corps zone made logistic support particularly difficult, and the intermixing of Army and Marine units created additional complications. The situation

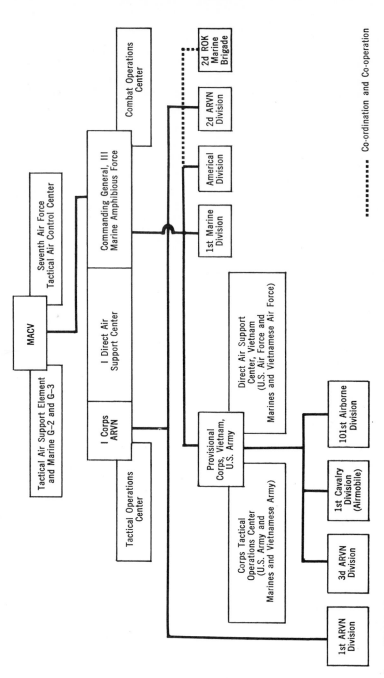

------- Co-ordination and Co-operation

there produced unusual command arrangements for supporting U.S. forces. Logistic support in Vietnam was organized on an area basis. In the I Corps area, the commander of U.S. Naval Forces, Vietnam, was responsible for common item support, base development (excluding U.S. Air Force bases), and real estate services for all U.S. and Free World forces. Furthermore, he provided logistic support for military operations at ports and beaches as well as items peculiar to Navy and Coast Guard support.

These responsibilities were carried out by the Naval Supply Activity at Da Nang. In addition, General Cushman supplied items needed exclusively by Marine units in the I Corps area. General Westmoreland, as commanding general of U.S. Army, Vietnam, was responsible for the supply of common items in the other three corps zones. Although Secretary of Defense McNamara had directed in late 1966 that plans be developed for the Army to assume common supply support responsibility throughout South Vietnam, agreement on procedures acceptable to all services had not been achieved. With the buildup of Army forces in the I Corps zone, however, Navy and Marine facilities could no longer meet the increased demand, so U.S. Army, Vietnam, had to expand logistic support efforts into this area. The Da Nang Support Command was established as a major element of the 1st Logistical Command to direct the sixty-five Army support units that USARV deployed to the I Corps area. Five of these units provided direct support to the Navy and Marines, and nine assumed some of the Navy's responsibilities, such as an over-the-beach logistic operation at Thon My Thuy. While the logistic support operations in the I Corps area during this period were efficiently carried out, they were accomplished through a complicated control arrangement involving Army, Navy, and Marine headquarters.

Naval Forces, Vietnam

At the end of 1965 the commanding general of the III Marine Amphibious Force was the tactical commander of Marine forces in the I Corps Tactical Zone as well as the senior adviser to the Vietnamese commanding general there. He was also the Navy component commander at MACV headquarters and was therefore charged with area co-ordination, logistic support, and base development. In order to ease the burden of the Marine commander, General Westmoreland recommended to Admiral Sharp, Commander in Chief, Pacific, that a Navy command be established in Vietnam. Consequently, on 1 April 1966, U.S. Naval Forces, Vietnam, was established with Rear Admiral Norvell G. Ward as commander. Naval Forces, Vietnam, assumed command of the Navy units in South Vietnam and, although assigned to the Pacific Fleet, was placed under the operational control of General Westmoreland. Concurrently, the III Marine Amphibious Force, together with its organic and assigned units, was designated a single service command assigned to the Fleet Marine Force, Pacific, and was placed under the operational control of General Westmoreland.

Mobile Riverine Force

In 1966 a concept was developed for extending U.S. combat power into the Mekong Delta area where the enemy was strong and where the United States had lacked the resources to assist the Vietnamese Army in achieving control. MACV headquarters organized what was originally called the Mekong Delta Mobile Afloat Force, soon to be known as the Mobile Riverine Force. The original plan called for basing one U.S. Army division in a location where it could operate along the Mekong and Bassac Rivers. Army troops were to be supported by U.S. Navy river assault groups, and one brigade of the division would be stationed aboard converted LSTs (landing ships, tank). This concept required new and unusual command relationships.

General Westmoreland proposed that one brigade of the arriving 9th Infantry Division be the Army component of a mobile joint task force. The Navy component would consist of tactical and logistic ships and craft to support the brigade afloat on riverine operations. General Westmoreland further proposed that the joint task force be commanded by the assistant commander of the 9th Division, who would have a small joint staff of operations, logistics, and communications personnel.

In Honolulu General Waters, Commander in Chief, U.S. Army, Pacific, concurred with General Westmoreland's proposal. Admiral Sharp and the commander in chief of the Pacific Fleet, however, favored a command arrangement in which the naval force would be under the operational control of the commander of the River Patrol Force (a task force, CTF 116, which was already conducting operations in the Mekong Delta) and would operate in support of the ground forces involved. A compromise solution ultimately developed, which placed U.S. Army units conducting riverine operations in the III and IV Corps Tactical Zones under the operational control of the commanding general of II Field Force. He could exercise control through a designated subordinate headquarters, such as the 9th Infantry Division. According to this arrangement, Navy units would be under the operational control of Admiral

CHART 9—COMMAND RELATIONS FOR RIVERINE OPERATIONS

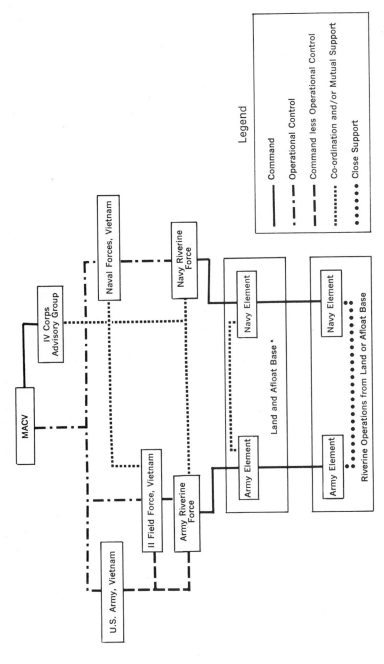

Legend

——— Command

—·—·— Operational Control

——— Command less Operational Control

············· Co-ordination and/or Mutual Support

•••••• Close Support

U.S. Army, Vietnam

MACV

IV Corps Advisory Group

Naval Forces, Vietnam

II Field Force, Vietnam

Army Riverine Force

Navy Riverine Force

Army Element

Navy Element

Land and Afloat Base [a]

Army Element

Navy Element

Riverine Operations from Land or Afloat Base

[a] The Army will provide the base commander both ashore and afloat. The Navy will provide its appropriate share of personnel for local base defense and primary efforts directed toward provision of gunfire support and protection against waterborne threats.

Source: CINCPAC Command History, 1966, Vol. II, p. 620.

Ward, who could also operate through a designated subordinate Navy commander. (Another task force, CTF 117, was established to control Navy riverine forces.) Finally, riverine operations would be conducted with Army and Navy units commanded separately, but the Navy would provide close support through procedures of mutual co-ordination. (*Chart 9*)

The Mobile Riverine Force began operations on 1 June 1967 with Operation CORONADO in Dinh Tuong Province. The 2d Brigade of the 9th Infantry Division and the Mobile Riverine Force conducted a two-month offensive in the vast waterways of the Mekong Delta with extraordinary success. The force continued aggressive operations until 25 August 1969, when the riverine force was deactivated and its mission and equipment were taken over by the Vietnamese Navy Amphibious Task Force 211.

Additional Military Assistance Commands

The enemy's 1968 *Tet* offensive revealed serious weaknesses in the Vietnamese organization for the defense of the Saigon area. For example, the commanding general of the Vietnamese III Corps had the basic responsibility for the capital, but he had no control over National Police units in his area. During the *Tet* offensive emergency, General Cao Van Vien, the chairman of the Joint General Staff, temporarily assumed command of all Vietnamese forces, including the National Police, within the Capital Military District. No permanent structure was established, however, and when the enemy resumed his attacks in May, the III Corps commanding general assumed personal command of all forces in the Saigon area. In June 1968 Major General Nguyen Van Minh was designated Military Governor of Saigon and of the adjoining Gia Dinh Province. Under the operational control of the III Corps commander, General Minh was given primary responsibility for the defense of the capital and control of all Vietnamese government forces charged with the security of Saigon and Gia Dinh. These forces included the Army of the Republic of Vietnam, the General Reserve, Regional and Popular Forces, the National Police, and the Military Police in the district. The Vietnamese Army commander of the Capital Military District became his deputy.

Corresponding adjustments were made on the U.S. side. During the *Tet* offensive, a command group from the II Field Force had moved to Saigon. This temporary headquarters, called Hurricane Forward, controlled all U.S. forces in the Saigon–Gia Dinh area and had the mission of advising the Vietnamese armed forces there. In May, Hurricane Forward was reconstituted and dispatched to

Saigon. The headquarters was redesignated Task Force Hay (for Major General John H. Hay, Jr., Deputy Commanding General, II Field Force, Vietnam). On 4 June 1968, this temporary arrangement became permanent, and General Hay was officially appointed senior adviser to General Minh, the Military Governor, and commander of U.S. forces defending Saigon and Gia Dinh. The forward headquarters was designated Capital Military Assistance Command, with the mission to plan and execute the defense of the Saigon–Gia Dinh area in coordination with the commanders

GENERAL ECKHARDT

of the U.S. Seventh Air Force and Naval Forces, Vietnam, and the Vietnamese Military Governor of Saigon–Gia Dinh. This move significantly strengthened the U.S. and Vietnamese organization for the defense of the Saigon capital area.

In another development, the senior adviser to the IV Corps Tactical Zone, Major General George S. Eckhardt, on 8 April 1969, assumed as an additional duty the position of Commanding General, Delta Military Assistance Command. The Delta Military Assistance Command was established to control the various U.S. Army units based in the delta area, including the U.S. 9th Infantry Division.

U.S. Army Logistical Advisory Effort

In May 1966 General Westmoreland asked Lieutenant General Jean E. Engler, Deputy Commanding General, U.S. Army, Vietnam, to study whether USARV headquarters should assume the Army's logistical advisory functions, which at the time were being performed by MACV's J-4 section, the Logistics Directorate. After completion of his survey, General Engler made several observations and recommendations. The entire Army military assistance and advisory effort should, he contended, be the exclusive function of U.S. Army, Vietnam, freeing the Military Assistance Command to concentrate on the control of its components. General Engler concluded that MACV was no longer operating as a military assistance command in the true sense of the term, since U.S. tactical

GENERAL PALMER. (*Photograph taken after his promotion to four-star general.*)

forces had been so greatly increased and their mission expanded. The newly instituted practice of funding military assistance programs through the individual services had further changed MACV's role. General Engler maintained that logistics should not be separated from operations and advisory activities, and therefore these functions should be performed by U.S. Army, Vietnam, in an expanded role as a full-fledged Army component.

As a result of General Engler's appraisal, logistic advisory functions were transferred to USARV headquarters, but the broader question of USARV's status was not resolved. Lieutenant General Bruce Palmer, Jr., who succeeded General Engler on 1 July 1967, elevated the logistic advisory group within the USARV staff to a general staff section, which he designated the Military Assistance Section. This action was prompted by General Palmer's conviction that logistic advisory responsibilities were equal in importance to the mission of supporting U.S. troops.

In the summer of 1967 a study called Project 640 was conducted by the Military Assistance Command. Its purpose was to examine the problems that had arisen because the MACV organization lacked a single staff focal point to co-ordinate and monitor all aspects of the assistance effort. As a result of the study, General Westmoreland established the post of Assistant Chief of Staff, Military Assistance, in the MACV staff to provide that focus. He also appointed a temporary committee to determine what functions could be transferred between MACV and USARV headquarters. On the committee's recommendation, logistic advisory functions were transferred from U.S. Army, Vietnam, back to the Military Assistance Command in February 1968.

Summary and Conclusions

During the period from mid-1966 to mid-1969 the authorized strength of U.S. forces in South Vietnam rose from about 276,000

CHART 10—TACTICAL GROUND FORCES

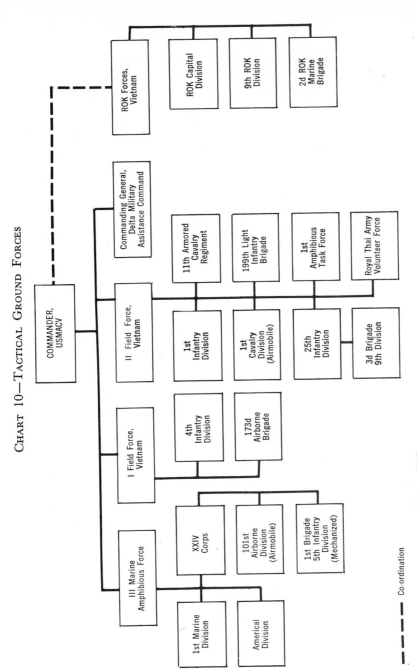

Source: USMACV Command History, 1969, Vol. I, p. IV–5.

men to a peak of 549,000. In June 1969, President Nixon announced from Midway Island the first of the U.S. force withdrawals, and graduated reductions continued from then on.

By the end of 1969 the control structure of major tactical ground forces was essentially the same as the one developed during 1965 and 1966. (*Chart 10*) The 1966–1969 period was not marked by basic structural changes in the chain of command. The modifications that were made were evolutionary and consistent with tactical requirements and expanded command responsibilities. By establishing the Civil Operations and Rural Development Support, U.S. civil and military efforts in support of Vietnamese pacification were at last united under General Westmoreland, the single manager. After the U.S. Army's XXIV Corps was deployed in the I Corps Tactical Zone, which used to be the Marine Corps' exclusive area, command arrangements were developed to control and support the combined efforts of Army and Marine forces. In the IV Corps Tactical Zone of the Mekong Delta, command arrangements were devised for directing joint Army-Navy operations of the Mobile Riverine Force. Finally, the Capital Military Assistance Command was organized to support the Vietnamese Saigon–Gia Dinh Capital Military District. MACV's command and control structure during the period from mid-1966 to mid-1969 thus proved to be flexible and strong enough to adjust not only to the doubling of U.S. forces in Vietnam, but also to the expanded tactical and logistic requirements, as well as to the added mission of managing the Civil Operations and Rural Development Support. The established command organization also held the promise of being able to cope with the phased reduction of U.S. forces in South Vietnam, which began in the summer of 1969, and with the complicated process of gradually turning over the war effort to the Vietnamese.

CHAPTER V

Model for the Future

No conflict in recent history has divided the American nation as much as the war in Vietnam. This study does not attempt to analyze the controversies surrounding the war or the psychological factors bearing on it or questions of U.S. foreign policy. However, since military planners must develop doctrine that can be applied in future military contingencies, lessons learned in Vietnam can be helpful. Some of these lessons concern theory and doctrine on effective command and control structures.

Military doctrine presupposes political decisions at the highest national level, which take into account the objectives and available means of military action. The planners use doctrine as a blueprint and apply it to the particular set of circumstances. These circumstances include the status of political relations between the United States and the country receiving assistance, the stability and effectiveness of the country's government, and the estimated magnitude, intensity, and duration of a U.S. military commitment. Obviously, these factors will influence the type of command organization selected to control U.S. military operations.

Command and control arrangements must meet other, more specific criteria. From the U.S. viewpoint, command and control must be comprehensive enough to exercise control over all military forces assigned by U.S. national authorities; flexible enough to respond to changes in the situation, such as a demand for specific control of air or naval operations in support of ground forces; and able to provide national authorities with timely, accurate, and complete reports. The command and control structure must also be capable of close co-operation with and constructive support of indigenous and allied military forces, paramilitary organizations, and other agencies of the host country.

In applying lessons learned in Vietnam to a hypothetical future conflict, the commitment of substantial contingents of U.S., allied, and indigenous forces for an extended period of time will be assumed. Further assumptions will be that U.S. objectives include an early conclusion of hostilities on terms favorable to the host government, that the conflict is limited to predetermined geographical and political areas, and that indigenous forces are to be strengthened, thus enabling them to assume responsibility for internal security. This example is not to be interpreted as a replica of the conflict in Indochina, nor do the following suggestions imply criticism of the command and control arrangements of the war in Vietnam.

The doctrine for command and control in this hypothetical case will be based on the premise that the conflict is classified as a single war, not one divided into separate geographical zones and by individual service missions. Another prerequisite will be unity of command, to ensure both tight control of the over-all U.S. effort by American political authorities and effectiveness of military operations and advisory activities. The command structure should encourage improvements in the operational capabilities of the indigenous forces and promote co-operation with them. Finally, the command and control arrangements should be sufficiently flexible to adjust to changes during the course of the war.

Given these premises, the optimum command and control structure would include the following recommendations.

1. A unified theater command directly under the Joint Chiefs of Staff should be established to conduct military operations. Other unified or specified commands may be assigned supporting missions depending on the type of conflict. The theater commander should have powers comparable to those exercised by supreme commanders in Europe and the Pacific during World War II.

2. Initially, the unified command (theater headquarters) should exercise operational control over forces provided by the host government. This command should also have operational control over military forces furnished by allied nations. The prototype of this arrangement is found in the Korean War. As an alternative, the unified command might only exercise control of U.S. and other outside forces committed to the theater. The degree of control over indigenous forces could be modified according to political circumstances but should be great enough to ensure prompt development of the ability of these forces to undertake unilateral operations successfully.

3. Combined operational and planning staffs should be established at the theater level and at major subordinate operating commands. A combined planning group, headed by an officer of the host government and staffed by representatives of the governments providing forces in the theater, is considered the best means of bringing the over-all effort together. An example of a combined staff is the Supreme Headquarters of the Allied Expeditionary Force in World War II.

4. Component headquarters, subordinate to the unified (theater) headquarters, should exercise both command and operational control over the forces of their respective U.S. services, especially since component headquarters are in fact responsible for logistical support. The service component headquarters should translate broad operational and policy guidance from the theater headquarters into specific plans and programs. This procedure follows the joint doctrine of United Action Armed Forces.

5. The component headquarters should exercise command and operational control over their elements of the Military Assistance Advisory Group assigned to the theater. The theater headquarters would have a separate, joint staff section to provide policy guidance to the service components concerning their advisory and assistance activities. A precedent for this type of arrangement was established during the Korean War.

6. Intermediate operational headquarters under the service components, such as field force or corps, provide a necessary command level for control of land combat operations. If indigenous or allied forces are operating within the tactical zone of a field force or corps, headquarters should be modified to function as combined staffs. Joint staffs at the field force level would only be needed under special circumstances, for example, if the combat zone was geographically isolated or if Marine and Army units were operating in the same area.

7. An organization like the Civil Operations and Rural Development Support (CORDS) in Vietnam should be established as soon as possible. It should directly control all civilian advisory efforts, especially those of the Central Intelligence Agency and the Joint United States Public Affairs Office. Without such control, civil affairs and counterinsurgency and pacification operations cannot be adequately co-ordinated. The functions of a CORDS-type organization could best be controlled through an arrangement similar to the one specified for Military Assistance Advisory Group activities.

8. Operational control of combat support and combat service support units needed on a day-to-day basis should be exercised by the intermediate field force or corps headquarters. Control of all other combat support and combat service support units should be retained by the Army component headquarters on the single-manager principle. This arrangement should apply specifically to Army air, engineer, signal, and medical units.

9. For common items of supply and services, logistical support should be provided according to a single-manager principle agreed upon by the four services. (*Chart 11*)

CHART 11—PROPOSED COMMAND AND CONTROL ARRANGEMENTS

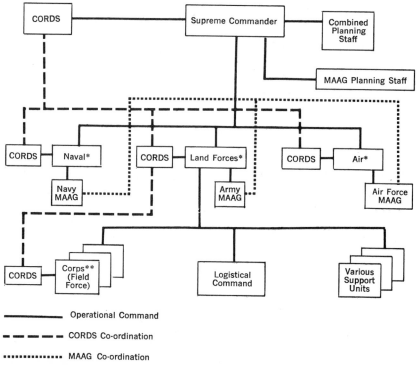

———————— Operational Command

— — — — — CORDS Co-ordination

••••••••••••••• MAAG Co-ordination

* Includes U.S., indigenous, and Free World forces

** Includes Marine Corps units

In Vietnam the doctrine of command and control drew heavily on historical precedent, but its application tended to be more complex than it had been in the past and became more involved as the mission of the U.S. command expanded. Looking to the future, contingencies of the magnitude and complexity of the Vietnam War cannot be ruled out. Should the United States again feel compelled to commit military forces, the need for a simple, well-defined, and flexible command structure on the U.S. side may conflict with the intricacies of indigenous political and military institutions and customs. Therefore, any future U.S. military assistance to foreign nations must be predicated on clear, mutually acceptable agreements, on a straight and direct line of authority among U.S. military and civilian assistance agencies, on full integration of all U.S. efforts, and on the ability to motivate the host country's armed forces and governmental agencies to fight and win.

Appendix

KEY U.S. OFFICIALS AND COMMANDERS IN VIETNAM, 1950–1969

Organization or Command	Official or Commander	Date of Assumption of Command
U.S. Legation	Edmund A. Gullion	17 Feb 50
	Donald R. Heath	6 Jul 50
U.S. Embassy	Donald R. Heath	25 Jun 52
	G. Frederick Reinhardt	10 May 55
	Elbridge Durbrow	20 Mar 57
	Frederick E. Nolting	21 Apr 61
	Henry Cabot Lodge	14 Aug 63
	Maxwell D. Taylor	2 Jul 64
	Henry Cabot Lodge	12 Aug 65
	Ellsworth Bunker	12 Apr 67
U.S. Military Assistance Advisory Group, Indochina	Brigadier General Francis G. Brink, USA	10 Oct 50
	Major General Thomas J. H. Trapnell, USA	1 Aug 52
	Lieutenant General John W. O'Daniel, USA	12 Apr 54
U.S. Military Assistance Advisory Group, Vietnam	Lieutenant General John W. O'Daniel, USA	12 Feb 54
	Lieutenant General Samuel T. Williams, USA	24 Oct 55
	Lieutenant General Lionel C. McGarr, USA	1 Sep 60
	Major General Charles J. Timmes, USA	1 Jul 62
U.S. Military Assistance Command, Vietnam	General Paul D. Harkins, USA	8 Feb 62
	General William C. Westmoreland, USA	20 Jun 64
	General Creighton W. Abrams, USA	2 Jul 68

Organization or Command	Official or Commander	Date of Assumption of Command
Deputy Commander, U.S. Military Assistance Command, Vietnam	Lieutenant General William C. Westmoreland, USA	27 Jan 64
	Lieutenant General John L. Throckmorton, USA	2 Aug 64
	Lieutenant General John A. Heintges, USA	5 Nov 65
	General Creighton W. Abrams, USA	1 Jun 67
	General Andrew J. Goodpaster, USA	3 Jul 68
	General William B. Rosson, USA	1 May 69
U.S. Army Support Group, Vietnam	Colonel Marvin H. Merchant, USA	3 Apr 62
	Brigadier General Joseph W. Stilwell, USA	26 Aug 62
U.S. Army Support Command, Vietnam	Brigadier General Joseph W. Stilwell, USA	1 Mar 64
	Brigadier General Delk M. Oden, USA	1 Jul 64
	Brigadier General John Norton, USA	1 Apr 65
U.S. Army, Vietnam	General William C. Westmoreland, USA	20 Jul 65
	General Creighton W. Abrams, USA	2 Jul 68
Deputy Commanding General, U.S. Army, Vietnam	Brigadier General John Norton, USA	20 Jul 65
	Lieutenant General Jean E. Engler, USA	24 Jan 66
	Lieutenant General Bruce Palmer, Jr., USA	1 Jul 67
	Lieutenant General Frank T. Mildren, USA	22 Jun 68
Commander, 2d Air Division	Lieutenant General Joseph H. Moore, USAF	31 Jan 64

Organization or Command	Official or Commander	Date of Assumption of Command
Commander, Seventh Air Force, Deputy Commander Air Operations, Military Assistance Command, Vietnam	Lieutenant General Joseph H. Moore, USAF	2 Apr 66
	General William W. Momyer, USAF	1 Jul 66
	General George S. Brown, USAF	1 Aug 68
Chief, U.S. Naval Advisory Group, Vietnam	Rear Admiral Norvell G. Ward, USN	10 May 65
Commander, U.S. Naval Forces, Military Assistance Command, Vietnam	Rear Admiral Norvell G. Ward, USN	1 Apr 66
	Rear Admiral Kenneth L. Veth, USN	27 Apr 67
	Vice Admiral Elmo B. Zumwalt, USN	30 Sep 68
Deputy Commander for CORDS	Ambassador Robert W. Komer	28 May 67
	Ambassador William E. Colby	8 Nov 68
Senior Advisor, I Corps, Commanding General, III Marine Amphibious Force	Major General William R. Collins, USMC	6 May 65
	Lieutenant General Lewis W. Walt, USMC	5 Jun 65
	Lieutenant General Robert E. Cushman, USMC	1 Jun 67
	Lieutenant General Herman Nickerson, Jr., USMC	26 Mar 69
Commanding General, Field Force, Vietnam	Major General Stanley R. Larsen, USA	25 Sep 65
Senior Advisor, II Corps, Commanding General, I Field Force, Vietnam	Lieutenant General Stanley R. Larsen, USA	15 Mar 66
	Lieutenant General William B. Rosson, USA	1 Aug 67
	Lieutenant General William R. Peers, USA	1 Mar 68
	Lieutenant General Charles A. Corcoran, USA	15 Mar 69

Organization or Command	Official or Commander	Date of Assumption of Command
Senior Advisor, III Corps, Commanding General, II Field Force, Vietnam	Lieutenant General Jonathan O. Seaman, USA	15 Mar 66
	Lieutenant General Bruce Palmer, Jr., USA	24 Mar 67
	Lieutenant General Frederick C. Weyand, USA	1 Jul 67
	Lieutenant General Walter T. Kerwin, Jr., USA	1 Aug 68
	Lieutenant General Julian J. Ewell, USA	2 Apr 69
Senior Advisor, IV Corps, Delta Military Assistance Command	Colonel George Barton, USA	17 Sep 64
	Brigadier General William R. Desobry, USA	3 Jun 66
	Major General George S. Eckhardt, USA	14 Jan 68
	Major General Roderick Wetherill, USA	1 Jun 69
Commanding General, Provisional Corps, Vietnam, XXIV Corps	Lieutenant General William B. Rosson, USA	10 Mar 68
	Lieutenant General Richard G. Stilwell, USA	15 Aug 68
	Lieutenant General Melvin Zais, USA	26 Jun 69
Senior Advisor, Commanding General, Capital Military Assistance Command	Major General John H. Hay, USA	8 Mar 68
	Major General Fillmore K. Mearns, USA	3 Aug 68
	Major General Walter B. Richardson, USA	13 Apr 69
	Brigadier General Charles J. Girard, USA	7 Nov 69

Glossary

AFFE	Army Forces, Far East (U.S.)
AFPAC	Army Forces in the Pacific (U.S.)
ARVN	Army of the Republic of Vietnam
CINCPAC	Commander in Chief, Pacific (U.S.)
CORDS	Civil Operations and Rural Development Support
COSSAC	Chief of Staff to the Supreme Allied Commander
ETOUSA	European Theater of Operations, U.S. Army
EUSAK	Eighth U.S. Army, Korea
FEC	Far East Command
MAAG	Military Assistance Advisory Group
MACTHAI	Military Assistance Command, Thailand
MACV	Military Assistance Command, Vietnam
MAP	Military Assistance Program
NATO	North Atlantic Treaty Organization
RD	Revolutionary Development (Vietnam)
RDSD	Revolutionary Development Support Directorate
ROK	Republic of Korea
SEATO	Southeast Asia Treaty Organization
TERM	Temporary Equipment Recovery Mission
TRIM	Training Relations and Instruction Mission
USAFFE	U.S. Army Forces in the Far East
USARV	U.S. Army, Vietnam
USARYIS	U.S. Army, Ryukyu Islands
USMACTHAI	U.S. Military Assistance Command, Thailand
USMACV	U.S. Military Assistance Command, Vietnam

Index